Federal
Admini

Aeronautical Information Services

Aeronautical Chart
Users' Guide

Effective as of 19 May 2022

TABLE OF CONTENTS

TABLE OF CONTENTS

TABLE OF CONTENTS

INTRODUCTION

This Chart Users' Guide is an introduction to the Federal Aviation Administration's (FAA) aeronautical charts and publications. It is useful to new pilots as a learning aid, and to experienced pilots as a quick reference guide.

The FAA is the source for all data and information utilized in the publishing of aeronautical charts through authorized publishers for each stage of Visual Flight Rules (VFR) and Instrument Flight Rules (IFR) air navigation including training, planning, and departures, enroute (for low and high altitudes), approaches, and taxiing charts. Digital charts are available online at:

- VFR Charts
- IFR Charts
- Terminal Procedures Publication
- Chart Supplements

Paper copies of the charts are available through an FAA Approved Print Provider. A complete list of current providers is available at http://www.faa.gov/air_traffic/flight_info/aeronav/print_providers/.

The FAA Aeronautical Information Manual (AIM) Pilot/Controller Glossary defines in detail, all terms and abbreviations used throughout this publication. Unless otherwise indicated, miles are nautical miles (NM), altitudes indicate feet above Mean Sea Level (MSL), and times used are Coordinated Universal Time (UTC).

Notices to Air Missions (NOTAMs) alert pilots to time-critical aeronautical information that is either temporary or not sufficiently known in advance to permit publication on aeronautical charts or in other operational publications. Pilots can access NOTAM information via Flight Service Stations (FSS) or online via NOTAM Search at https://notams.aim.faa.gov/notamSearch/.

In addition to NOTAMs, the Safety Alerts/Charting Notices page of the Aeronautical Information Services website is also useful to pilots.

KEEP YOUR CHARTS CURRENT

Aeronautical information changes rapidly, so it is important that pilots check the effective dates on each aeronautical chart and publication. To avoid danger, it is important to always use current editions and discard obsolete charts and publications.

To confirm that a chart or publication is current, refer to the next scheduled edition date printed on the cover. Pilots should also check NOTAMs for important updates between chart and publication cycles that are essential for safe flight.

EFFECTIVE DATE OF CHART USERS' GUIDE AND UPDATES

All information in this guide is effective as of **19 May 2022**. All graphics used in this guide are for educational purposes. Chart symbology may not be to scale. Please do not use them for flight navigation.

The Chart Users' Guide is updated when there is new chart symbology or when there are changes in the depiction of information and/or symbols on the charts. It will be published in accordance with the 56-day aeronautical chart product schedule.

COLOR VARIATION

Although the digital files are compiled in accordance with charting specifications, the final product may vary slightly in appearance due to differences in printing techniques/processes and/or digital display techniques.

REPORTING CHART DISCREPANCIES

Your experience as a pilot is valuable and your feedback is important. We make every effort to display accurate information on all FAA charts and publications, so we appreciate your input. Please notify us concerning any requests for changes, or potential discrepancies you see while using our charts and related products.

FAA, Aeronautical Information Services
1305 East-West Highway
SSMC4, Room 3424
Silver Spring, MD 20910-3281

Telephone Toll-Free 1-800-638-8972
Aeronautical Inquires: https://www.faa.gov/air_traffic/flight_info/aeronav/aero_data/Aeronautical_Inquiries/

WHAT'S NEW?
Update as of 19 May 2022

The following charting items have been added to the Chart Users' Guide since the Guide was last published on 24 March 2022:

VFR CHARTS

No Significant Changes Applied

— —

IFR ENROUTE CHARTS

No Significant Changes Applied

— —

TERMINAL PROCEDURE PUBLICATION (TPP)

Compulsory NAVAID, reporting point, and waypoint symbols have been removed from the Instrument Approach Procedure (IAP) Planview Legend page. There has never been a requirement for their usage in the Terminal environment.

In order to provide additional clarity for Required Navigation Performance (RNP) profiles, a new example of an RNP profile with annotated Track-to-Fix (TF) and Radius-to-Fix (RF) segments has been added to the Profile View section and to the Terminal Procedures Publication (TPP) Profile View Legend page.

EXPLANATION OF VFR TERMS AND SYMBOLS

This chapter covers the Sectional Aeronautical Chart (Sectional). These charts include the most current data at a scale of (1:500,000) which is large enough to be read easily by pilots flying by sight under Visual Flight Rules. Sectionals are named after a major city within its area of coverage.

The chart legend includes aeronautical symbols and information about drainage, terrain, the contour of the land, and elevation. You can learn to identify aeronautical, topographical, and obstruction symbols (such as radio and television towers) by using the legend.

A brief description next to a small black square indicates the exact location for many of the landmarks easily recognized from the air, such as stadiums, pumping stations, refineries, etc. A small black open circle with descriptive type indicates oil, gas or mineral wells. A small black circle with descriptive type indicates water, oil or gas tanks. The scale for some items may be increased to make them easier to read on the chart.

Aeronautical Information Services' charts are prepared in accordance with specifications of the Interagency Air Committee (IAC) and are approved by representatives of the Federal Aviation Administration (FAA) and the Department of Defense (DoD).

WATER FEATURES (HYDROGRAPHY)

Water features are depicted using two tones of blue, and are considered either "Open Water" or "Inland Water." "Open Water," a lighter blue tone, shows the shoreline limitations of all coastal water features at the average (mean) high water levels for oceans and seas. Light blue also represents the connecting waters like bays, gulfs, sounds and large estuaries.

Exceptionally large lakes like the Great Lakes, Great Salt Lake, and Lake Okeechobee, etc., are considered Open Water features. The Open Water tone extends inland as far as necessary to adjoin the darker blue "Inland Water" tones. All other bodies of water are marked as "Inland Water" in the darker blue tone.

LAND FEATURES (TERRAIN) AND OBSTRUCTIONS

The elevation and configuration of the Earth's surface is important to pilots. Our Aeronautical Information Specialists are devoted to showing the contour of the earth and any obstructions clearly and accurately on our charts. We use five different techniques: contour lines, shaded relief, color tints, obstruction symbols, and Maximum Elevation Figures (MEF).

1. Contour lines join points of equal elevation. On Sectionals, basic contours are spaced at 500' intervals. Intermediate contours are typically at 250' intervals in moderately level or gently rolling areas. Auxiliary contours at 50', 100', 125', or 150' intervals occasionally show smaller relief features in areas of relatively low relief. The pattern of these lines and their spacing gives the pilot a visual concept of the terrain. Widely spaced contours represent gentle slopes, while closely spaced contours represent steep slopes.

2. Shaded relief shows how terrain may appear from the air. Shadows are shown as if light is coming from the northwest, because studies have shown that our visual perception has been conditioned to this view.

3. Different color tints show bands of elevation relative to sea level. These colors range from light green for the lower elevations, to dark brown for the higher elevations.

4. Obstruction symbols show man made vertical features that could affect safe navigation. FAA's Aeronautical Information Manual (AIM) maintains a database of over obstacles in the United States, Canada, the Caribbean, Mexico and U.S. Pacific Island Territories. Aeronautical Specialists evaluate each obstacle based on charting specifications before adding it to a visual chart. When a Specialist is not able to verify the position or elevation of an obstacle, it is marked UC, meaning it is "under construction" or being reported, but has not been verified.

The FAA uses a Digital Obstacle File (DOF) to collect and disseminate data. Because land and obstructions frequently change, the source data on obstructions and terrain is occasionally incomplete or not accurate enough for use in aeronautical publications. For example, when the FAA receives notification about an obstruction, and there is insufficient detail to determine its position and elevation, the FAA Flight Edit Program conducts an investigation.

The Flight Edit crew visually verifies the cultural, topographic, and obstacle data. Charts are generally flight-checked every four years. This review includes checking for any obstruction that has been recently built, altered, or dismantled without proper notification.

Obstacles less than 1000' AGL. Sectional Charts, Terminal Area (TACs) and Caribbean Charts (CACs) typically show man-made obstacles extending more than 200' Above Ground Level (AGL), or more than 299' AGL in yellow city tint. Features considered to be hazardous obstacles to low-level flight are; smokestacks, tanks, factories, lookout towers, and antennas, etc.

Obstacles 1000' AGL or greater.

5540
(650)

GARFIELD STACK

Man-made features used by FAA Air Traffic Control as checkpoints use a graphic symbol shown in black with the required elevation data in blue. The elevation of the top of the obstacle above Mean Sea Level (MSL) and the height of the structure (AGL) is also indicated (when known or can be reliably determined by a Specialist). The AGL height is in parentheses below the MSL elevation. In extremely congested areas, the FAA typically omits the AGL values to avoid confusion.

4977
(1432)

Group Obstacle Symbol

Whenever possible, the FAA depicts specific obstacles on charts. However, in high-density areas like city complexes, only the highest obstacle is represented on the chart using the group obstacle symbol to maximize legibility.

5000
(1500) UC

If space is available, the AGL height of the obstruction is shown

Obstacles under construction are indicated by placing the letters UC adjacent to the obstacle type.

Guy wires may extend outward from obstacles.

Obstacles with high-intensity strobe lighting systems may operate part-time or by proximity activation and are shown as follows:

5. The Maximum Elevation Figure (MEF) represents the highest elevation within a quadrant, including terrain and other vertical obstacles (towers, trees, etc.). A quadrant on Sectionals is the area bounded by ticked lines dividing each 30 minutes of latitude and each 30 minutes of longitude. MEF figures are rounded up to the nearest 100' value and the last two digits of the number are not shown.

12⁵

In this example the MEF represents 12,500'.

19633
GLACIER

12000

9000

7000

5000

3000

2000

1000

Sea Level

-228

MEFs over land and open water areas are used in areas containing man-made obstacles such as oil rigs.

In the determination of MEFs, the FAA uses extreme care to calculate the values based on the existing elevation data shown on source material. Aeronautical Information Specialists use the following procedure to calculate MEFs:

MEF - Man-made Obstacle

When a man-made obstacle is more than 200' above the highest terrain within the quadrant:

1. Determine the elevation of the top of the obstacle above MSL.

2. Add the possible vertical error of the source material to the above figure (100' or 1/2 contour interval when interval on source exceeds 200'. U.S. Geological Survey Quadrangle Maps with contour intervals as small as 10' are normally used).

3. Round the resultant figure up to the next higher hundred-foot level.

Example:

Elevation of obstacle top (MSL)	2649
Possible obstacle error	+100
equals	2749
Raise to the following 100' level	2800
Maximum Elevation Figure (MEF)	28

MEF - Natural Terrain Feature or Natural Vertical Obstacle

When a natural terrain feature or natural vertical obstacle (e.g. a tree) is the highest feature within the quadrangle:

1. Determine the elevation of the feature.

2. Add the possible vertical error of the source to the above figure (100' or 1/2 the contour interval when interval on source exceeds 200').

3. Add a 200' allowance for uncharted natural or manmade obstacles. Chart specifications don't require the portrayal of obstacles below minimum height.

4. Round the figure up to the next higher hundred-foot level.

Example:

Elevation of obstacle top (MSL)	13161
Possible vertical error	+100
Obstacle Allowance	+200
equals	13461
Raise to the following 100' level	13500
Maximum Elevation Figure (MEF)	13⁵

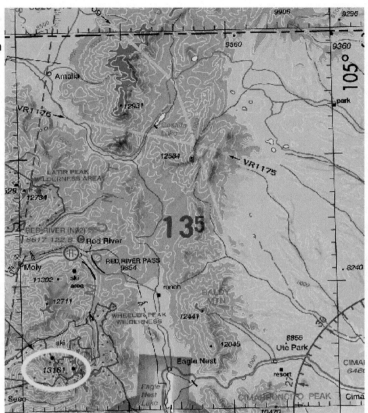

Pilots should be aware that while the MEF is based on the best information available to the Specialist, the figures are not verified by field surveys. Also, users should consult the Aeronautical Information Services website to ensure that your chart has the latest MEF data available.

LAND FEATURES - MOUNTAIN PASSES

Mountain Pass symbol does not indicate a recommended route or direction of flight and pass elevation does not indicate a recommended clearnce altitude. Hazardous flight conditions may exist within and near mountain passes.

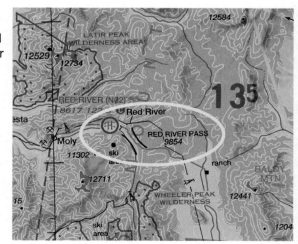

RADIO AIDS TO NAVIGATION

On VFR Charts, information about radio aids to navigation (NAVAID) are boxed, as illustrated. Duplication of data is avoided. When two or more radio aids in a general area have the same name with different frequencies, Tactical Air Navigation (TACAN) channel numbers, or identification letters, and no misinterpretation can result, the name of the radio aid may be indicated only once within the identification box. Very High Frequency/Ultra High Frequency (VHF/UHF) NAVAID names and identification boxes (shown in blue) take precedence. Only those items that differ (e.g., frequency, Morse Code) are repeated in the box in the appropriate color. The choice of separate or combined boxes is made in each case on the basis of economy of space and clear identification of the radio aids.

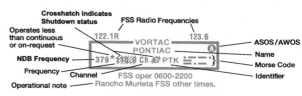

A NAVAID that is physically located on an airport may not always be represented as a typical NAVAID symbol. A small open circle indicates the NAVAID location when collocated with an airport icon.

The type of NAVAID will be identified by: "VOR," (VHF Omni-Directional Range) "VORTAC" (VOR Tactical Aircraft Control), "VOR-DME," (VOR-Distance Measuring Equipment) or "DME" (Distance Measuring Equipment) positioned on and breaking the top line of the NAVAID box.

DMEs are shown without the compass rose.

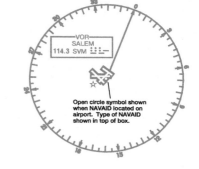

AIRPORTS

Airports in the following categories are charted as indicated (additional symbols are shown later in this Section). Public use airports:

 Hard-surfaced runways greater than 8069' or some multiple runways less than 8069'

 Hard-surfaced runways 1500' to 8069'

 ○ Other than hard-surfaced runways

 Seaplane bases

Military airports:

 ◎   ◎ Other than hard-surfaced runways

Hard-surfaced runways are depicted the same as public-use airports.

U.S. military airports are identified by abbreviations such as AAF (Army Air Field), AFB (Air Force Base), MCAS (Marine Corps Air Station), NAS (Naval Air Station), NAV (Naval Air Facility), NAAS (Naval Auxiliary Air Station), etc. Canadian military airports are identified by the abbreviation DND (Department of National Defense).

Fuel Available:

  Fuel availability indicated by use of tick marks around the basic airport symbol. Consult Chart Supplement for details and availability.

Other airports with or without fuel:

 Ⓗ Ⓕ Ⓤ Ⓡ ⊗

15

Airports are plotted in their true geographic position unless the symbol conflicts with a NAVAID at the same location. In such cases, the airport symbol will be displaced, but the relationship between the airport and the NAVAID will be retained. When depicting a seaplane base, the eye of the anchor symbol will be charted as close to the docking area as possible, with the remainder of the symbol in the water.

Airports are identified by their designated name. Generic parts of long airport names (such as "airport," "field," or "municipal") and the first names of persons are commonly omitted unless they are needed to distinguish one airport from another with a similar name.

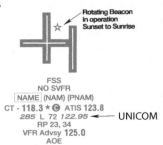

The elevation of an airport is the highest point on the usable portion of the landing areas. Runway length is the length of the longest active runway, including displaced thresholds and excluding overruns. Runway length is shown to the nearest 100', using 70 as the rounding point; a runway 8070' in length is charted as 81, while a runway 8069' in length is charted as 80. If a seaplane base is collocated with an airport, there will be additional seaplane base water information listed for the elevation, lighting and runway.

Flight Service Station on field	FSS	Elevation in feet	285
Airports where fixed wing special VFR operations are prohibited (shown above airport name) FAR 91	NO SVFR	Lighting in operation Sunset to Sunrise	L
Indicates FAR 93 Special Air Traffic Rules and Airport Traffic Pattern	▭	Lighting limitations exist; refer to Chart Supplement	*L
Location Identifier	(NAM)	Length of longest runway in hundreds of feet; usable length may be less	72
ICAO Location Identifier	(PNAM)	Aeronautical advisory station	122.95
Control Tower (CT) - primary frequency	CT - 118.3	Runways with Right Traffic Patterns (public use)	RP 23,34
Star indicates operation part-time. See tower frequencies tabulation for hours of operation	★	See Chart Supplement	*RP
Follows the Common Traffic Advisory Frequency (CTAF)	Ⓒ	VFR Advisory Service Shown when ATIS is not available and frequency is other than the primary CT frequency	VFR Advsy 125.0
Automatic Terminal Information Services	ATIS 123.8	Weather Camera (Alaska)	WX CAM
Automatic Flight Information Service	AFIS 135.2	Airport of Entry	AOE
Automated Surface Weather Observing Systems; shown when full-time ATIS is not available	ASOS/AWOS 135.42	When information is lacking, the respective character is replaced by a dash. Lighting codes refer to runway edge lights and may not represent the longest runway or full length lighting.	

Airports with Control Towers (CT) and their related data are shown in blue. All other airports and their related data are shown in magenta. The L symbol indicates that runway lights are on from dusk to dawn. *L indicates that the pilot must consult the Chart Supplement to determine runway lighting limitations, such as: available on request (by radio-call, letter, phone, etc), part-time lighting, or pilot/airport controlled lighting. Lighting codes refer to runway edge lights. The lighted runway may not be the longest runway available, and lights may not be illuminated along the full length of the runway. The Chart Supplement has a detailed description of airport and air navigation lighting aids for each airport. A dash represents no runway edge lights.

The symbol ☆ indicates the existence of a rotating or flashing airport beacon operating from dusk to dawn. The Aeronautical Information Manual (AIM) thoroughly explains the types and uses of airport lighting aids.

Right traffic information is shown using the abbreviation 'RP' for right pattern, followed by the appropriate runway number(s) (RP 18). Special conditions or restrictions to the right pattern are indicated by the use of an asterisk (*RP) to direct the pilot to the Chart Supplement for special instructions and/or restrictions.

The type "OBJECTIONABLE" associated with an airport symbol indicates that an objectionable airspace determination has been made for the airport per FAA JO 7400.2 Section 4, Airport Charting and Publication of Airport Data. Objectionable airspace determinations are based upon a number of factors including conflicting traffic patterns with another airport, hazardous runway conditions, or natural or man-made obstacles in close proximity to the landing area. FAA Regional Airports Offices are responsible for airspace determinations. Address any challenges to objectionable airspace determinations to your FAA Regional Airports Office.

AIRSPACE

CONTROLLED AIRSPACE

Controlled airspace consists of those areas where some or all aircraft may be subject to air traffic control, such as: Class A, Class B, Class C, Class D, Class E Surface (SFC) and Class E Airspace.

Class A Airspace within the United States extends from 18,000' up to FL600. While visual charts do not depict Class A, it is important to note its existence.

Class B Airspace is shown in abbreviated form on the Caribbean Charts (CAC) . The Sectional Aeronautical $\;\;$ *Class B MSL* $\overline{\underset{}{90}}$ Chart (Sectional) and Terminal Area Chart (TAC) show Class B in greater detail. The MSL ceiling and floor alti- $\;$ *Altitudes* $\;20$ tudes of each sector are shown in solid blue figures with the last two zeros omitted. Floors extending "upward from above" a certain altitude are preceded by a (+). Operations at and below these altitudes are outside of Class B Airspace. Radials and arcs used to define Class B are prominently shown on TACs. Detailed rules and requirements associated with the particular Class B are shown. The name by which the Class B is shown as LAS VEGAS CLASS B for example.

Class C Airspace is shown in abbreviated form on Caribbean Charts (CAC). Sectionals and TACs show $\;\;$ *Class C MSL* $\overline{\underset{}{70}}$ Class C in greater detail. The MSL ceiling and floor altitudes of each sector are shown in solid magenta $\;$ *Altitudes* $\;15$ figures with the last two zeros eliminated.

$\dfrac{T}{SFC}$ The figure at left identifies a sector that extends from the surface to the base of the Class B.

Class C Airspace is identified by name: BURBANK CLASS C

Separate notes, enclosed in magenta boxes, give the approach control frequencies to be used by arriving VFR aircraft to establish two-way radio communication before entering the Class C (generally within 20 NM): CTC BURBANK APP WITHIN 20 NM ON 124.6 395.9

Class C operating less than continuous is indicated by the following note: See NOTAMs/Supplement for Class C eff hrs

Class D Airspace is identified with a blue dashed line. Class D operating less than continuous is indicated by the following note: See NOTAMs/Supplement for Class D eff hrs

Ceilings of Class D are shown as follows: ⌐30⌐

A minus in front of the figure is used to indicate "from surface to, but not including..."

Class E Surface (SFC) Airspace is symbolized with a magenta dashed line. Class E (SFC) operating less than continuous is indicated by the following note: See NOTAMs/Supplement for Class E (sfc) eff hrs

Class E Airspace exists at 1200' AGL unless designated otherwise. The lateral and vertical vertical limits of all Class E, (up to, but not including 18,000') are shown by narrow bands of vignette on Sectionals and TACs.

CLASS G Class E Airspace with floor 700 ft. above surface that laterally abuts Class G Airspace.
Class E Airspace with floor 700 ft. above surface that laterally abuts 1200 ft. or higher Class E Airspace
Class E Airspace with floor 1200 ft. or greater above surface that laterally abuts Class G Airspace

Controlled airspace floors of 700' above the ground are defined by a magenta vignette; floors other than 700' that laterally abut uncontrolled airspace (Class G) are defined by a blue vignette; differing floors greater than 700' above the ground are annotated by a symbol and a number indicating the floor. 2400 AGL
4500 MSL

If the ceiling is less than 18,000' MSL, the value (preceded by the word "ceiling") is shown along the limits of the controlled airspace. These limits are shown with the same symbol indicated above.

UNCONTROLLED AIRSPACE

Class G Airspace within the United States extends up to 14,500' Mean Sea Level. At and above this altitude is Class E, excluding the airspace less than 1500' above the terrain and certain special use airspace areas.

SPECIAL USE AIRSPACE

Special Use Airspace (SUA) confines certain flight activities and restricts entry, or cautions other aircraft operating within specific boundaries. Except for Controlled Firing Areas, SUA areas are depicted on VFR Charts. Controlled Firing Areas are not charted because their activities are suspended immediately when spotter aircraft, radar, or ground lookout positions indicate an aircraft might be approaching the area. Nonparticipating aircraft are not required to change their flight paths. SUA areas are shown in their entirety (within the limits of the chart), even when they overlap, adjoin, or when an area is designated within another area. The areas are identified by type and identifying name/number, and are positioned either within or immediately adjacent to the area.

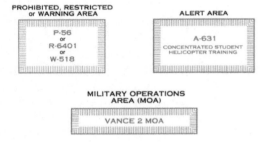

* Alert Areas do not extend into Class A, B, C and D airspace, or Class E airport surface areas.

OTHER AIRSPACE AREAS

Mode C Required Airspace (from the surface to 10,000' MSL) within a 30 NM radius of the primary airport(s) for which a Class B is designated, is depicted by a solid magenta line.

Mode C is required, but not depicted for operations within and above all Class C up to 10,000' MSL.

Enroute Mode C requirements (at and above 10,000' MSL except in airspace at and below 2500' AGL) are not depicted. See FAR 91.215 and the AIM.

FAR 93 Airports and heliports under Federal Aviation Regulation 93 (FAR 93), (Special Air Traffic Rules and Airport Traffic Patterns), are shown by "boxing" the airport name.

FAR 91 Airports where fixed wing special visual flight rules operations are prohibited (FAR 91) are shown with the type "NO SVFR" above the airport name.

National Security Areas indicated with a broken magenta line ▬ ▬ ▬ and Special Flight Rules Areas (SFRAs) indicated with the following symbol: ▬ ▬ ▬ , consist of airspace with defined vertical and lateral dimensions established at locations where there is a requirement for increased security and safety of ground facilities. Pilots should avoid flying through these depicted areas. When necessary, flight may be temporarily prohibited.

The Washington DC Flight Restricted Zone (FRZ) is related to National Security. It is depicted using the Prohibited/Restricted/Warning Area symbology ▨▨▨▨▨▨ and is located within the SFRA. It is defined as the airspace within approximately a 13 to 15 NM radius of the DCA VOR-DME. Additional requirements are levied upon aviators requesting access to operate inside the National Capital Region.

Temporary Flight Restriction (TFR) Areas Relating to National Security are indicated with a broken blue line ▬ ▬ ▬. A Temporary Flight Restriction (TFR) is a type of Notice to Air Missions (NOTAM). A TFR defines an area where air travel is restricted due to a hazardous condition, a special event, or a general warning for the entire airspace. The text of the actual TFR contains the fine points of the restriction. It is important to note that only TFRs relating to National Security are charted.

Air Defense Identification Zones (ADIZs) are symbolized using the ADIZ symbol: ▪▪▪▪▪▪▪▪▪▪▪▪▪. As defined in Code of Federal Regulations 14 (CFR 14) Part 99, an ADIZ is an area in which the ready identification, location, and control of all aircraft is required in the interest of national security. ADIZ boundaries include Alaska, Hawaii, Guam, Canada and the Contiguous U.S.

National Defense Airspace Temporary Flight Restriction (TFR) Areas are bounded with cross hatching: ///////////. These areas include airspace that is subject to routine TFRs published as NOTAMs that have a 12+ month duration.

Terminal Radar Service Areas (TRSAs) are shown in their entirety, symbolized by a screened black outline of the entire area including the various sectors within the area ▭▭▭▭▭▭.

The outer limit of the entire Terminal Radar Service Areas (TRSA) is a continuous screened black line. The various sectors within the TRSA are symbolized by narrower screened black lines.

Each sector altitude is identified in solid black color by the MSL ceiling and floor values of the respective sector, eliminating the last two zeros. A leader line is used when the altitude values must be positioned outside the respective sectors because of charting space limitations. The TRSA name is shown near the north position of the TRSA as follows: **PALM SPRINGS TRSA**. Associated frequencies are listed in a table on the chart border.

Military Training Routes (MTRs) are shown on Sectionals and TACs. They are identified by the route designator: ——← IR21 ——. Route designators are shown in solid black on the route centerline, positioned along the route for continuity. The designator IR or VR is not repeated when two or more routes are established over the same airspace, e.g., IR201-205-227. Routes numbered 001 to 099 are shown as IR1 or VR99, eliminating the initial zeros. Direction of flight along the route is indicated by small arrowheads adjacent to and in conjunction with each route designator.

The following note appears on Helicopters, Sectionals and TACs except for Hawaiian Islands which is different.

MILITARY TRAINING ROUTES (MTRs)

All IR and VR MTRs are shown, and may extend from the surface upwards. Only the route centerline, direction of flight along the route, and the route designator are depicted - route widths and altitudes are not shown.

DoD users refer to Area Planning AP/1B Military Training Routes North and South America for current routes.

There are IFR (IR) and VFR (VR) routes as follows:

Route identification:

    a. Routes at or below 1500' AGL (with no segment above 1500') are identified by four-digit numbers; e.g., VR1007, etc. These routes are generally developed for flight under Visual Flight Rules.

    b. Routes above 1500' AGL (some segments of these routes may be below 1500') are identified by three or fewer digit numbers; e.g., IR21, VR302, etc. These routes are developed for flight under Instrument Flight Rules.

MTRs can vary in width from 4 to 16 miles. Detailed route width information is available in the Flight Information Publication (FLIP) AP/1B (a Department of Defense publication), or through the 56 Day NASR Subscription from the National Flight Data Center (NFDC).

Special Military Activity areas are indicated on Sectionals by a boxed note in black type. The note contains radio frequency information for obtaining area activity status.

**SPECIAL MILITARY ACTIVITY
CTC MOBILE RADIO
ON 123.6
FOR ACTIVITY STATUS**

TERMINAL AREA CHART (TAC) COVERAGE

TAC coverage is shown on appropriate Sectionals by a 1/4" masked line as indicated below. Within this area pilots should use TACs, which provide greater detail. A note indicating that the area is on the TAC appears near the masked boundary line.

════ LOS ANGELES TERMINAL AREA ════
Pilots are encouraged to use the Los Angeles VFR
Terminal Area Chart for flights at or below 10,000'

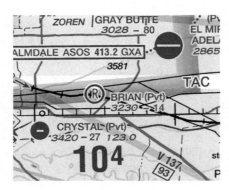

INSET AND SPECIAL CHART COVERAGE

Inset and Special Chart Coverage (.i.e., Grand Canyon Chart) is shown on appropriate Sectionals by a 1/8" masked line as indicated below. A note to this effect appears near the masked boundary line. (Additional examples shown in VFR Sectional and Terminal Charts > Navigational and Procedural Information > Chart Limits.)

If inset chart is on the same chart as outline:

════ INDIANAPOLIS INSET ════
See inset chart for additional detail

If inset chart is on a different chart:

════ INDIANAPOLIS INSET ════
See inset chart on the St. Louis
Sectional for additional information

CHART TABULATIONS

Airport Tower Communications are provided in a columnized tabulation for all tower-controlled airports that appear on the respective chart. Airport names are listed alphabetically. If the airport is military, the type of airfield, e.g., AAF, AFB, NAS, is shown after the airfield name. In addition to the airport name, tower operating hours, primary Very High Frequency/Ultra High Frequency (VHF/UHF) local Control Tower (CT), Ground Control (GND CON), and Automatic Terminal Information Service (ATIS) frequencies, when available, will be given. Airport Surveillance Radar (ASR) and/or Precision Approach Radar (PAR) procedures are listed when available.

Approach Control Communications are provided in a columnized tabulation listing Class B, Class C, Terminal Radar Service Areas (TRSA) and Selected Approach Control Facilities when available. Primary VHF/UHF frequencies are provided for each facility. Sectorization occurs when more than one frequency exists and/or is approach direction dependent. Availability of service hours is also provided.

Special Use Airspace (SUA): Prohibited, Restricted and Warning Areas are presented in blue and listed numerically for U.S. and other countries. Restricted, Danger and Advisory Areas outside the U.S. are tabulated separately in blue. A tabulation of Alert Areas (listed numerically) and Military Operations Areas (MOA) (listed alphabetically) appear on the chart in magenta. All are supplemented with altitude, time of use and the controlling agency/contact facility, and its frequency when available. Users need to be aware that a NOTAM addressing activation will NOT be issued to announce permanently listed times of use. The controlling agency will be shown when the contact facility and frequency data is unavailable.

Airports with control towers are indicated on the face of the chart by the letters CT followed by the primary VHF tower frequency(ies). Information for each tower is listed in the table below. Operational hours are local time. The primary VHF and UHF tower and ground control frequencies are listed.

Automatic Terminal Information Service (ATIS) frequencies shown on the face of the chart are arrival VHF/UHF frequencies. All ATIS frequencies are listed in the table below. ATIS operational hours may differ from tower operational hours.

ASR and/or PAR indicate Radar Instrument Approach available.

"MON-FRI" indicates Monday through Friday.

O/T indicates other times.

Frequencies (VHF/UHF)

CONTROL TOWER	OPERATES	TOWER	GND CON	ATIS	ASR/PAR
AIRBORNE	0700 MON-1800 SAT 0600-1800 SUN	119.475	121.6	124.925	
BLUE GRASS	CONTINUOUS	119.1 257.8	121.9	126.3	
BOLTON	0730-1930	128.1	121.3 (E) 121.8 (W)		ASR/PAR
CHARLOTTESVILLE-ALBEMARLE	0600-2300	124.5 338.275	121.9 338.275	118.425	PAR
CINCINNATI/NORTHERN KENTUCKY INTL	CONTINUOUS	118.3 (RWYS 18R/36L & 09/27) 118.975 360.85 (RWY 18L/36R)	121.3 (E) 121.7 (W)	134.375 (ARR) 135.3 (DEP)	ASR
COX DAYTON INTL	CONTINUOUS	119.9 257.8	121.9	125.8	
EASTERN WV RGNL/ SHEPHERD	0700-2200 TUE-THU 0700-1600 FRI-SAT 1300-1800 SUN O/T BY NOTAM	124.3 236.6	121.8 275.8		

Airport Name

Runway dependent

Hours of Operation (local time)

Approach direction dependent

Radar Instrument Approach available

Frequencies (VHF/UHF)

CLASS B, CLASS C, TRSA AND SELECTED RADAR APPROACH CONTROL FREQUENCIES

FACILITY	FREQUENCIES		SERVICE AVAILABILITY
CINCINNATI CLASS B	VHF UHF	119.7 (RWY 09/27 090°-269°) (RWY 18L/36L 180°-359°) 123.875 (RWY 09/27 270°-089°) (RWY 18L/36R 360°-179°) 363.15	CONTINUOUS
CHARLESTON CLASS C		124.1 269.125 (N) 119.2 269.125 (S)	CONTINUOUS
COLUMBUS CLASS C		120.2 317.775 (280°-099°) 132.3 279.6 (100°-279°)	CONTINUOUS
DAYTON CLASS C		127.65 294.5 (360°-090°) 118.85 327.1 (091°-180°) 134.45 316.7 (181°-359°)	CONTINUOUS
BRISTOL TRSA		134.425 349.0 (047°-227°) 125.5 317.5 (228°-046°) O/T 127.85 371.85 ZTL CNTR	0600-2400
HUNTINGTON TRSA		119.75 257.8 (S) 132.95 257.8 (N)	CONTINUOUS
PERKINSON/BAAF RADAR		118.75 353.9	CONTINUOUS

O/T indicates Other times

Airspace Name

Radar Approach Control

Sectors for VHF and UHF traffic

local time

SPECIAL USE AIRSPACE ON SECTIONAL CHART

Unless otherwise noted altitudes are MSL and in feet. Time is local.
"TO" an altitude means "To and including."
FL – Flight Level
NO A/G – No air to ground communications. Contact nearest FSS for information.

† Other times by NOTAM.
NOTAM – Use of this term in Restricted Areas indicates FAA and DoD NOTAM systems. Use of this term in all other Special Use areas indicates the DoD NOTAM system.

U.S. P–PROHIBITED, R–RESTRICTED, W–WARNING, A–ALERT, MOA–MILITARY OPERATIONS AREA

NUMBER	ALTITUDE	TIME OF USE	CONTROLLING AGENCY/ CONTACT FACILITY	FREQUENCIES —— VHF/UHF
R-6602 A	TO BUT NOT INCL 4000	CONTINUOUS MAY 1-SEP 15 †24 HRS IN ADVANCE	WASHINGTON CNTR	118.75 377.1
R-6602 B	4000 TO BUT NOT INCL 11,000	BY NOTAM 24 HRS IN ADVANCE	WASHINGTON CNTR	118.75 377.1
R-6602 C	11,000 TO BUT NOT INCL 18,000	BY NOTAM 24 HRS IN ADVANCE	WASHINGTON CNTR	118.75 377.1
A-220	TO 4000 AGL	0800-2200	NO A/G	

Alert Areas do not extend into Class A, B, C and D airspace, or Class E airport surface areas.

MOA NAME	ALTITUDE*	TIME OF USE†	CONTROLLING AGENCY/ CONTACT FACILITY	FREQUENCIES —— VHF/UHF
BRUSH CREEK	100 AGL TO BUT NOT INCL 5000	0800-2200 MON-SAT	INDIANAPOLIS CNTR	134.0 135.57
BUCKEYE	5000	0800-2200 MON-FRI 0800-1600 SAT-SUN	INDIANAPOLIS CNTR	134.0 135.57
EVERS	1000 AGL	SR-SS BY NOTAM	WASHINGTON CNTR	

*Altitudes indicate floor of MOA. All MOAs extend to but do not include FL 180 unless otherwise indicated in tabulation or on chart.
†Other times by DoD NOTAM.

Sunrise to Sunset

CANADA R–RESTRICTED, D–DANGER AND A–ADVISORY AREA

NUMBER	LOCATION	ALTITUDE	TIME OF USE	CONTROLLING AGENCY
CYR754	CONFEDERATION BRIDGE, PE	TO 500	CONTINUOUS	
CYD734	HALIFAX, NS	TO FL 200	OCCASIONAL BY NOTAM	MONCTON ACC
CYA702 (P)	GREENWOOD, NS	TO 500	CONT DAYLIGHT	
CYA752 (M)	LIVERPOOL, NS	TO FL 280	CONT DAYLIGHT MON-FRI EXC HOL†	MONCTON ACC

Restricted
Danger
Advisory

CARIBBEAN VFR AERONAUTICAL CHARTS (CAC)

Starting in 2016, the FAA CARIBBEAN VFR Aeronautical Charts were first published, replacing the discontinued World Aeronautical Charts (WACs), parts of CH-25, CJ-26, and CJ-27, with CJ-26's last effective date of 1 February 2018 and CJ-27 last effective date of 29 March 2018. The Caribbean Charts are published as two VFR Charts: Caribbean 1 (CAC-1) covers Southern Florida, Cuba, Haiti and the Bahamas; Caribbean 2 (CAC-2) covers Puerto Rico, Haiti, Dominican Republic, the Lesser Antilles and Leeward Islands. CAC-1 is updated annually and CAC-2 biennially.

Caribbean Charts are designed for VFR and provide aeronautical and topographic information of the Caribbean. The aeronautical information includes airports, radio aids to navigation, Class B airspace and special use airspace. The topographic information includes city tint, populated places, principal roads, drainage patterns and shaded relief.

The chart symbols used on the Caribbean Charts are similar to those used in the Sectional and Terminal Area Charts, the major difference being in scale. The Caribbean VFR Chart scale is 1:1,000,000 vs the Sectional Chart Scale of 1:500,000 and Terminal Area Chart Scale of 1:250,000. Chart symbology will appear smaller on the Caribbean VFR Charts.

Example from Caribbean 1 VFR Aeronautical Chart

Airport Traffic Service and Airport Space Information Unique to CAC

Only airway and reserved airspace effective below 18,000' MSL in the U.S. airspace and below FL200 outside of the U.S. airspace are shown.

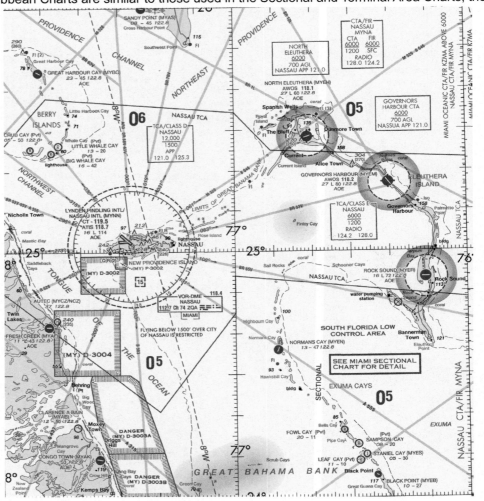

VFR SECTIONAL AND TERMINAL AREA CHARTS

GENERAL INFORMATION

The symbols shown in this section illustrate those that appear in the Sectional Aeronautical Charts (Sectionals) and Terminal Area Charts (TACs). The same symbology is utilized in VFR Flyway Planning Charts, Helicopter Route Charts and Caribbean Aeronautical Charts (CACs), however the scale of the symbols may be different due to the particular chart scales. Where symbology is distinctive to a given chart, examples and explanations are given in the additional examples.

AIRPORTS

Landplane: Civil

	Non-Towered	Towered

Airports having control towers (CT) are shown in blue, all others are shown in magenta.

All recognizable runways, including some which may be closed, are shown for visual identification purposes. Fuel available.

Runway patterns will be depicted at airports with at least one hard surfaced runway 1500′ or greater in length.

Landplane: Civil-Military

	Non-Towered	Towered

Landplane: Military

	Non-Towered	Towered

Refueling and repair facilities not indicated.

Heliport

	Non-Towered	Towered

(Selected)

Seaplane: Civil

	Non-Towered	Towered

Ultralight Flight Park

(Selected)

Landplane: Emergency / Landmark Value

Fuel not available

or

Complete information is not available.

Appropriate note as required for hard surfaced runways only: "(CLOSED)"

Seaplane: Emergency

Fuel not available or complete information is not available.

PUBLIC USE - (Soft surfaced runway, or hard surfaced runway less than 1500' in length.) Fuel not available.

RESTRICTED OR PRIVATE - (Soft surfaced runway, or hard surfaced runway less than 1500' in length.) Non-public use having emergency or landmark value.

OBJECTIONABLE

OBJECTIONABLE is an airport that has an airspace determination based upon a number of factors including conflicting traffic patterns with another airport, hazardous runway conditions, or natural or man-made obstacles in close proximity to the landing area.

UNVERIFIED - A landing area available but warranting more than ordinary precaution due to:

(1) lack of current information on field conditions,

and/or

(2) available information indicates peculiar operating limitations.

ABANDONED - Depicted for landmark value or to prevent confusion with an adjacent usable landing area. (Normally at least 3000' paved).

23

AIRPORTS (Continued)

Airport Data Grouping

(Pvt): Non-public use having emergency or landmark value.

"OBJECTIONABLE": This airport may adversely affect airspace use.

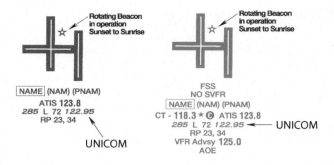

Flight Service Station on field	FSS
Airports where fixed wing special VFR operations are prohibited (shown above airport name) FAR 91	NO SVFR
Indicates FAR 93 Special Air Traffic Rules and Airport Traffic Pattern	⬜
Location Identifier	(NAM)
ICAO Location Identifier	(PNAM)
Control Tower (CT) - primary frequency	CT - 118.3
Star indicates operation part-time. See tower frequencies tabulation for hours of operation	★
Follows the Common Traffic Advisory Frequency (CTAF)	ⒸBVVV
Automatic Terminal Information Services	ATIS 123.8
Automatic Flight Information Service	AFIS 135.2
Automated Surface Weather Observing Systems; shown when full-time ATIS is not available.	ASOS/AWOS 135.42

Elevation in feet	285
Lighting in operation Sunset to Sunrise	L
Lighting limitations exist; refer to Chart Supplement	*L
Length of longest runway in hundreds of feet; usable length may be less.	72
Aeronautical advisory station	122.95
Runways with Right Traffic Patterns (public use)	RP 23,34
See Chart Supplement	*RP
VFR Advisory Service Shown when ATIS is not available and frequency is other than the primary CT frequency.	VFR Advsy 125.0
Weather Camera (Alaska)	WX CAM
Airport of Entry	AOE

When information is lacking. the respective character is replaced by a dash. Lighting codes refer to runway edge lights and may not represent the longest runway or full length lighting.

FAA Chart Users' Guide - VFR Symbology - Sectional and Terminal Area Charts

RADIO AIDS TO NAVIGATION

VOR

Operates less than contiuous or On-Request

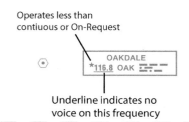

Underline indicates no voice on this frequency

VORTAC

When an NDB NAVAID shares the same name and Morse Code as the VOR NAVAID the frequency can be col-located inside the same box to conserve space.

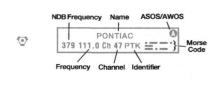

NDB Frequency · Name · ASOS/AWOS

PONTIAC
379 111.0 Ch 47 PTK — Morse Code

Frequency · Channel · Identifier

VOR-DME

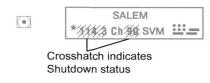

SALEM
114.3 Ch 90 SVM

Crosshatch indicates Shutdown status

DME

PROVO
Ch 21 PVU (108.4)

DME co-located at an airport
Note: DMEs are shown without the compass rose.

DME
SARGO
Ch 93 GVR (114.65)

Compass Rose

Compass Rose is "reference" oriented to magnetic north

Example of VOR NAVAID co-located at airport

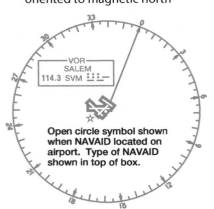

VOR
SALEM
114.3 SVM

Open circle symbol shown when NAVAID located on airport. Type of NAVAID shown in top of box.

Non-Directional Radio Beacon (NDB)

MONTAGUE
404 MOG

Underline indicates no voice on this frequency

NDB-DME

GAMBELL
369 GAM
DME Ch 92 (114.5)

NAVAID Used To Define Class B Airspace
ILS Components
ILS-DME

CLEVELAND-HOPKINS
DME ANTENNA
(I-HPI) Ch 36 (109.9)

TAC - Shown when used in description of Class B airspace.

SALT LAKE CITY DME ANTENNA
(I-BNT/I-UTJ) Ch 52 (111.5)

Compass Rosette

Shown only in areas void of VOR roses.

Compass rosette will be based on the five year epoch magnetic variation model.

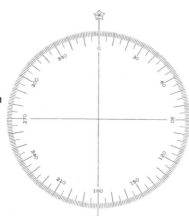

RADIO AIDS TO NAVIGATION (Continued)

Automated Weather Broadcast Services

Automated Weather Observing System (AWOS) / Automated Surface Observing System (ASOS).	VHF/UHF	LF/MF
		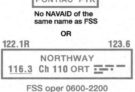

Flight Service Station (FSS)

Heavy line box indicates Flight Service Station (FSS). Frequencies 122.2 and 255.4 (Conterminous U.S.); 121.5, 122.2, 243.0 and 255.4 (Alaska); and 121.5, 126.7, and 243.0 (Canada) are available at many FSSs and are not shown above boxes. All other frequencies are shown. Frequencies transmit and receive except those followed by an R.

R - receive only

PONTIAC PTK
No NAVAID of the same name as FSS

OR

122.1R   123.6
NORTHWAY
116.3 Ch 110 ORT

FSS oper 0600-2200
Rancho Murieta FSS other times.

NAVAID same name as FSS
but not an RCO

Off Airport AWOS/ASOS

SANDBERG ASOS 120.625 SDB

Broadcast Stations (BS)

On request by the proper authority or when a VFR Checkpoint

KFTM

BS
KFTM
1400

Remote Communications Outlet (RCO)

Frequencies above thin line box are remoted to NAVAID site. Other frequencies at FSS providing voice communication may be available determined by altitude and terrain. Consult Chart Supplement for complete information.

Thin line box without frequencies and controlling FSS name indicates no FSS frequency available.

122.525   123.65
HANCOCK RCO
GREEN BAY

122.35
ST PAUL
108.6 STP
MINNEAPOLIS

FSS Radio
providing
voice
communications

122.35
HUMPHREY
275 HPY
MILES CITY

AIRSPACE INFORMATION

Class B Airspace

Sectional

LAS VEGAS CLASS B

Appropriate notes as required may be shown.

Only the airspace effective below 18,000 feet MSL are shown.

(Mode C see FAR 91.215 / AIM)

Terminal Area Chart (TAC)

LAS VEGAS CLASS B

LAS 20 NM

LAS 002°

CTC LAS VEGAS APP
ON 121.1 OR 257.8

All mileages are nautical (NM).

All radials are magnetic.

AIRSPACE INFORMATION (Continued)

Class C Airspace

Appropriate notes as required may be shown.

(Mode C see FAR 91.215/AIM)

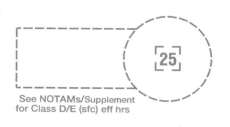

BURBANK CLASS C

See NOTAMs/Directory for Class C eff hrs

$\frac{48}{30}$ — Ceiling of Class C in hundreds of feet MSL
— Floor of Class C in hundreds of feet MSL

CTC BURBANK APP WITHIN 20 NM ON 124.6 395.9

Class D Airspace

Altitude in hundreds of feet MSL

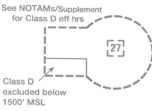

See NOTAMs/Supplement for Class D eff hrs

Class D excluded below 1500' MSL

(A minus in front of the figure is used to indicate "from surface to but not including...")

See NOTAMs/Supplement for Class D/E (sfc) eff hrs

Class E Airspace

The limits of Class E airspace shall be shown by narrow vignettes or by the dashed magenta symbol. Individual units of designated airspace are not necessarily shown; instead, the aggregate lateral and vertical limits shall be defined by the following:

See NOTAMs/Supplement for Class D/E (sfc) eff hrs

Airspace beginning at the surface (sfc) designated around airports..

Airspace beginning at 700 feet AGL that laterally abuts 1200 feet or higher Class E Airspace...

700' Class E eff 0600-2300

Airspace beginning at 700 feet AGL that laterally abuts uncontrolled (Class G) airspace...

CLASS G

Airspace beginning at 1200 feet AGL that laterally abuts uncontrolled (Class G) airspace...

Differentiates floors of airspace greater than 700 feet above the surface...

When the ceiling is less than 18,000 feet MSL, the value prefixed by the word "CEILING", shall be shown along the limits.

CEILING
14,000 MSL

8000 AGL

Airspace beginning at the surface (sfc) designated around airports...

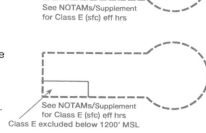

See NOTAMs/Supplement for Class E (sfc) eff hrs

Airspace beginning at the surface with an airspace exclusion area where Class E airspace is excluded below 1200' MSL.

See NOTAMs/Supplement for Class E (sfc) eff hrs
Class E excluded below 1200' MSL

AIRSPACE INFORMATION (Continued)

Class E Airspace (Continued)

Low Altitude Airways VOR and LF/MF (Class E Airspace)

Low altitude Federal Airways are indicated by centerline.

Only the controlled airspace effective below 18,000 feet MSL is shown

Miscellaneous Air Routes

Combined Federal Airway/RNAV 2 "T" Routes are identified in solid blue type adjacent to the solid magenta federal airway identification.

The joint route symbol is screened magenta.

Canadian Airspace

Individual units of designated Canadian airspace are not necessarily shown; instead, the aggregate lateral and vertical limits shall be portrayed as closely as possible to the comparable U.S. airspace.

Appropriate notes as required may be shown

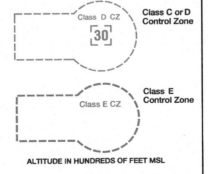

Flight Information Regions (FIR)

Oceanic Control Areas (OCA)

Control Areas (CTA)

Offshore Control Areas

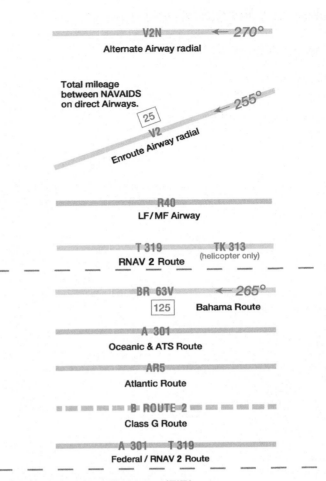

28

AIRSPACE INFORMATION (Continued)

Special Conservation Areas

National Park, Wildlife Refuge, Primitive and Wilderness Areas, etc.

NOAA Regulated National Marine Sanctuary Designated Areas

Flight operations below 1000' AGL over the designated areas within the Gulf of Farallones National Marine Sanctuary violate NOAA regulations (see 15 CFR 922).

Special Flight Rules Area (SFRA) Relating to National Security

Example: Washington DC

Appropriate notes as required may be shown.

Note: Delimiting line not shown when it coincides with International Boundary, projection lines or other linear features.

Washington DC Metropolitan Area Special Flight Rules Area/Flight Restricted Zone (DC SFRA & DC FRZ) (See description in Atlantic Ocean).

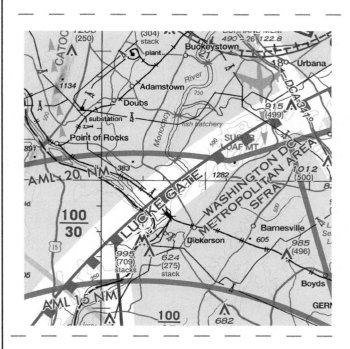

Temporary Flight Restriction (TFR) Relating to National Security

Example: Washington DC

Appropriate notes as required may be shown.

CAUTION
CONTACT FLIGHT SERVICE FOR LATEST FLIGHT RESTRICTION STATUS AND NOTAMS ASSOCIATED WITH P-40 AND R-4009

AIRSPACE INFORMATION (Continued)

Special Flight Rules Area (SFRA)

SPECIAL FEDERAL AVIATION REGULATIONS (SFAR)
14 CFR Part 93, Subpart U and SFAR 50.2 -
GRAND CANYON NATIONAL PARK SPECIAL
FLIGHT RULES AREA. Special regulations apply
to all aircraft operations below 18,000 feet MSL.

Special Use Airspace

Only the airspace effective below 18,000 feet MSL is shown.

The type of area shall be spelled out in large areas if space permits.

P-56
OR
R-6401
OR
W-518

PROHIBITED, RESTRICTED or WARNING AREA

* Alert Areas do not extend into Class A, B, C and D airspace, or Class E airport surface areas.

ALERT AREA
A-631

CONCENTRATED STUDENT
HELICOPTER TRAINING

ALERT AREA

VANCE 2 MOA

VANCE 2 MOA
EXCLUDES AIRSPACE
1500' AGL AND BELOW

MILITARY OPERATIONS AREA (MOA)

Special Air Traffic Rules / Airport Patterns (FAR Part 93)

Appropriate boxed note as required shown adjacent to area.

Inside the FAR Part 93 boundary area, the cross hatching is at a 45 degree angle. The hypsometric tint shall be masked within the area around the yellow city tint when applicable (should not be confused with white glacier tint).

SPECIAL NOTICE
Pilots are required to
obtain an ATC clearance
prior to entering this area.

Flight Restricted Zone (FRZ) Relating to National Security

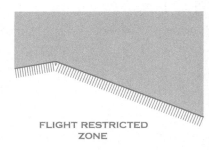

FLIGHT RESTRICTED ZONE

National Security Area

Appropriate notes as required may be shown

Small Area

NOTICE
FOR REASONS OF NATIONAL SECURITY
PILOTS ARE REQUESTED TO AVOID FLIGHT
BELOW 1200' MSL IN THIS AREA

Special Awareness Training Areas

DCA-VOR-DME-60 NM

NOTICE
Special awareness training required within 60 NM
of DCA VOR-DME. See description on Flyway.

Mode C (FAR 91.215)

Appropriate notes as required may be shown.

MODE C & ADS-B OUT
30 NM

Air Defense Identification Zone (ADIZ)

Note: Delimiting line not shown when it coincides with International Boundary, projection lines or other linear features.

CONTIGUOUS
U.S. ADIZ

AIRSPACE INFORMATION (Continued)

High Energy Radiation Areas

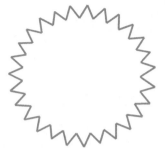

Appropriate notes as required may be shown.

Solar Farm-
Ocular Glare

Military Training Routes (MTR)

◄—VR269

Special Military Activity Routes (SMAR)

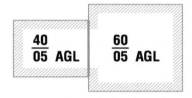

$\frac{40}{05}$ AGL $\frac{60}{05}$ AGL

Boxed notes shown adjacent to route.

SPECIAL MILITARY ACTIVITY
CTC ALBUQUERQUE CNTR ON 135.875
FOR ACTIVITY STATUS

$\frac{40}{05}$ AGL

IFR Routes

Arrival

15,000 - 7000

Departure

8000 - 12000

Arrival/Departure

IFR ARRIVALS   IFR DEPARTURES

8000 - 5000   5000 - 8000

TAC only

Special Security Notice Permanent Continuous Flight Restriction Areas

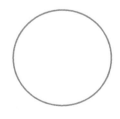

DISNEYLAND THEME PARK
See Note for requirements

Sporting Event Temporary Flight Restriction (TFR) Sites

 STADIUM

National Defense Airspace Temporary Flight Restriction (TFR) Areas

Dallas National
Defense Airspace TFR
Check NOTAMs

Space Operations Area (FAR Part 91.143)

DARKER TINT IS
FAR 91.143 AREA

Miscellaneous Activity Areas

Aerobatic Practice Area

Glider Operations

Hang Glider Activity

Ultralight Activity

Unmanned Aircraft Activity

Parachute Jumping Area with Frequency 122.9

Space Launch Activity Area

FAA Chart Users' Guide - VFR Symbology - Sectional and Terminal Area Charts

AIRSPACE INFORMATION (Continued)

VFR Transition Routes

Appropriate notes as required may be shown.

> VFR TRANSITION ROUTE
> ATC CLEARANCE REQUIRED
> SEE SHOWBOAT GRAPHIC
> ON SIDE PANEL

Uni-directional

Bi-directional

Bi-directional with NAVAID Ident and Radial

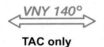

VNY 140°

TAC only

Examlple: Los Angeles

Terminal Radar Service Area (TRSA)

TRSA Name

HARRISBURG TRSA

TRSA Boundaries

TRSA Sectors

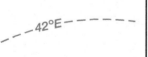

Appropriate notes as required may be shown.

80 - Ceiling of TRSA in hundreds of feet MSL
40 - Floor of TRSA in hundreds of feet MSL

> SEE TWR FREQ TAB

Example: Harrisburg, PA

NAVIGATIONAL AND PROCEDURAL INFORMATION

Isogonic Line and Value

Isogonic lines and values shall be based on the five year epoch magnetic variation model.

— — 42°E — — —

Local Magnetic Notes

Unreliability Notes

> Magnetic disturbance of as much as 78° exists at ground level and 10° or more at 3000 feet above ground level in this vicinity.

Intersections

Named intersections used as reporting points. Arrows are directed toward facilities which establish intersection.

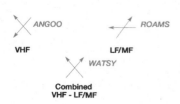

ANGOO

ROAMS

VHF

LF/MF

WATSY

Combined
VHF - LF/MF

Aeronautical Lights

By Request

Rotating or Oscillating

Isolated Location

Rotating Light with Flashing Code Identification Light

Rotating Light with Course Lights and Site Number

FAA Chart Users Guide - VFR Symbology - Sectional and Terminal Area Charts

NAVIGATIONAL AND PROCEDURAL INFORMATION (Continued)

Airport Beacons

Rotating or Flashing

Isolated Locations

☆ 2520

VFR Checkpoints

Underline indicates proper name of VFR Checkpoint.

Pictorial   STATE CAPITOL

■ SIGNAL HILL

Ⓡ LEWIS (Pvt)
989 - 27

NORTHBROOK
113.0 Ch 77 OBK

VFR Waypoints

RNAV

◇ GRANT

Stand-Alone

◆ VPXYZ

Collocated with VFR Checkpoint

NAME
(VPXYZ)

Obstruction

Above 200' & below 1000' AGL
(above 299' AGL in urban area)

Λ 1473
(394)
bldg

Under Construction (UC) or reported and
position/elevation unverified

Λ 628
UC

1000' and higher (AGL)

3368
(1529)

Wind Turbine

2179
(315)

High-Intensity Obstruction Lights

Less than 1000' (AGL)

1000' and higher (AGL)

Wind Turbine

Group obstruction

Wind Turbines

High-intensity lights may operate part-time
or by proximity activation.

Marine Lights

With Characteristics of Light

Oc
R SEC
●
Land Light

Red	R
White	•W
Green	G
Blue	BU
Orange	OR
Black	B
Yellow	Y
Sector	SEC
Fixed	F
Single Occulting	Oc
Group Occulting	Oc (2)
Composite Group Occulting	Oc (2+1)
Isophase	Iso
Flashing	Fl
Group Flashing	Fl (2)
Composite Group Flashing	Fl (2+1)
Quick	Q
Interrupted Quick/Interrupted Quick Flashing	IQ
Morse Code	Mo (A)
Fixed and Flashing	FFl
Alternating	Al
Group	Gp
Long Flash	LFl
Group Quick Flashing	Q (3)
Very Quick Flashing	VQ
Group Very Quick Flashing	VQ (3)
Interrupted Very Quick Flashing	IVQ
Ultra Quick Flashing	UQ
Interuppted Ultra Quick Flashing	IUQ

*** Marine Lights are white unless other-
wise noted. Alternating lights are red and white unless
otherwise noted.**

Group Obstruction

Above 200' & below 1000' AGL
(above 299' AGL in urban area)

1062
(227)

1000' and higher (AGL)

4977
(1432)

At least two in group
1000' and higher (AGL)

2889
(1217)

Wind Turbines

2735
(415)

Wind Turbine Farms

When highest wind turbine is unverified,
UC will be shown after MSL value.

2894' UC

Maximum Elevation Figure (MEF)

(see VFR Terms tab for explanation)

135

NAVIGATIONAL AND PROCEDURAL INFORMATION (Continued)

Chart Limits

Outline on Sectional of Terminal Area Chart

LOS ANGELES TERMINAL AREA
Pilots are encouraged to use the Los Angeles VFR
Terminal Area Chart for flights at or below 10,000'

Outline of Special Chart on Sectional and Terminal Area Chart

GRAND CANYON CHART

Outline on Sectional of Inset Chart

If inset chart is on the same chart as outline:

INDIANAPOLIS INSET
See inset chart for additional detail

If inset chart is on a different chart:

INDIANAPOLIS INSET
See inset chart on the St. Louis
Sectional for additional information

CULTURE

Railroads

Single Track

Double Track

More Than Two Tracks

3 tracks

Electric

electric

Non-operating, Abandoned or Under Construction

under construction

Roads

Dual-Lane Divided Highway
Category 1

Primary
Category 2

Secondary
Category 2

Trails

Category 3

Provides symbolization for dismantled railroad when combined with label "dismantled railroad."

Railroad Yards
Limiting Track To Scale

railroad yard

Location Only

railroad yard

Railroad Stations

station   station

Railroad Sidings and Short Spurs

Road Markers

Interstate Route No.

80

U.S. Route No.

40

Air Marked Identification Label

13

Road Names

LINCOLN HIGHWAY

Roads Under Construction

under construction

CULTURE (Continued)

Related Features to Railroads and Roads

Bridges and Viaducts

Railroad

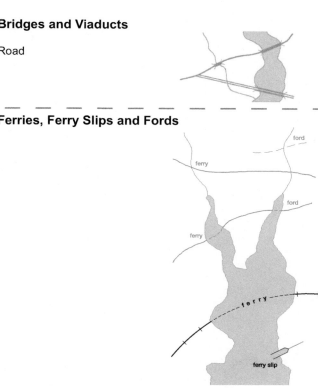

Causeways

Overpasses and Underpasses

Tunnels-Road and Railroad

Bridges and Viaducts

Road

Ferries, Ferry Slips and Fords

Populated Places

Yellow tinted areas indicate populated places.

Small circle indicates an area too small to depict using yellow tint.

ST LOUIS

Font Style and Size indicate the category of the populated area:

Large Cities Category 1
- population more than 250,000

Cities and Large Towns Category 2
- population 25,000 to 250,000

Towns and Villages Category 3
- population less than 25,000

ST LOUIS

NASHVILLE

Frankfort

CULTURE (Continued)

BOUNDARIES

International

State or Province

Convention or Mandate Line

RUSSIA

UNITED STATES

Time Zones

PST +8 (+7DT) = UTC

MST +7 (+6DT) = UTC

Date Line

INTERNATIONAL   (Monday)

DATE LINE   (Sunday)

Miscellaneous Cultural Features

Dams

Dam Carrying Road

Passable Locks

locks

Small Locks

Weirs and Jetties

jetties

Seawalls

seawall

Breakwaters

breakwater

breakwater

Piers, Wharfs, Quays, etc.

piers

piers

piers

Pipelines

pipeline

Underground

underground pipeline

**Power Transmission
and Telecommunication Lines**

Landmark Features

■ substation

■ fort

■ cemetery

Tanks

● water

● oil

● gas

Mines or Quarries

Shaft Mines or Quarries

Outdoor Theater

Wells

Other than water

○ oil

Race Tracks

Coast Guard Station

CG

Lookout Towers
(Elevation Base of Tower)

⊕
618

Landmark Areas

Aerial Cableways, Conveyors, Etc.

aerial cableway

landfill

HYDROGRAPHY

Open Water

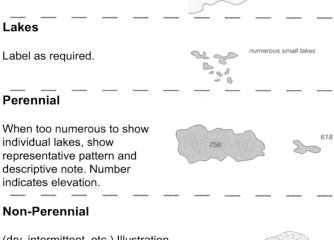

Open/Inland Water

Lakes

Label as required.

Perennial

When too numerous to show
individual lakes, show
representative pattern and
descriptive note. Number
indicates elevation.

Non-Perennial

(dry, intermittent, etc.) Illustration
includes small perennial lake.

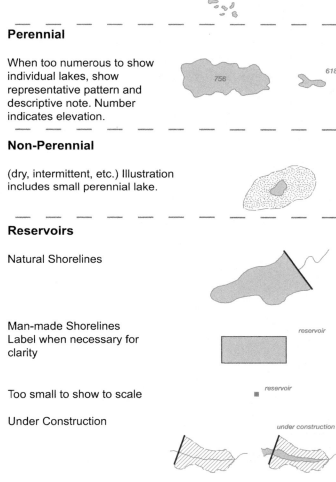

Reservoirs

Natural Shorelines

Man-made Shorelines
Label when necessary for
clarity

Too small to show to scale

Under Construction

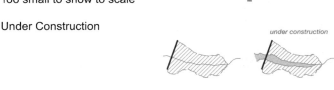

Inland Water

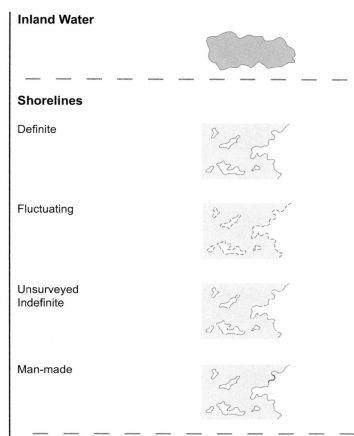

Shorelines

Definite

Fluctuating

Unsurveyed
Indefinite

Man-made

FAA Chart Users' Guide - VFR Symbology - Sectional and Terminal Area Charts

HYDROGRAPHY (Continued)

Streams

Perennial

Non-Perennial

Fanned Out

Alluvial fan

Braided

Disappearing

Seasonally Fluctuating

with undefined limits

with maximum bank limits, prominent and constant

Sand Deposits in and along riverbeds

Wet Sand Areas

Within and adjacent to desert areas

Aqueducts

To Scale

aqueduct

Abandoned or Under Construction

abandoned aqueduct

Underground

underground aqueduct

Falls

Double-Line

falls

Single-Line

falls

Canals

ERIE

To Scale

Abandoned or Under Construction

abandoned

Abandoned to Scale

abandoned

Small Canals and Drainage / Irrigation Ditches

Perennial

Non-Perennial

Abandoned or Ancient Numerous

abandoned

Representative pattern and/or descriptive note.

numerous canals and ditches

Suspended or Elevated

Tunnels

Kanats
Underground with Air Vents

underground aqueduct

Rapids

Double-Line

rapids

Single-Line

rapids

FAA Chart Users' Guide - VFR Symbology - Sectional and Terminal Area Charts

HYDROGRAPHY (Continued)

Salt Evaporators and Salt Pans Man Exploited

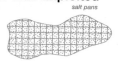

Hummocks and Ridges

Peat Bogs

Rice Paddies

Extensive areas indicated
by label only.

Springs, Wells and Waterholes

Permanent Snow and Ice Areas

Glaciers

Glacial Moraines

Ice Cliffs

Snowfields, Ice Fields And Ice Caps

Foreshore Flats

Tidal flats exposed at low tide.

Swamps, Marshes and Bogs

Mangrove And Nipa

Cranberry Bogs

Land Subject To Inundation

Tundra

Ice

Permanent
Polar Ice

Pack Ice

Ice Peaks

HYDROGRAPHY (Continued)

Reefs-Rocky or Coral

Fish Ponds and Hatcheries

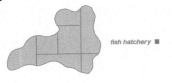

Miscellaneous Underwater Features Not Otherwise Symbolized

Wrecks

Exposed

Rocks-Isolated

Bare or Awash

RELIEF

Contours

Basic

Approximate

Intermediate

Auxiliary

Depression
(Illustration includes mound within depression)

Values

Sand or Gravel Areas

Sand Dunes

To Scale

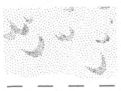

Hachuring

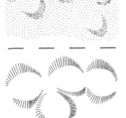

Spot Elevations

Position Accurate

Position Accurate, Elevation Approximate

Highest in General Area

Highest on Chart

Mountain Pass

Distorted Surface Areas

Lava Flows

Sand Ridges

To Scale

Shaded Relief

RELIEF (Continued)

Quarries To Scale

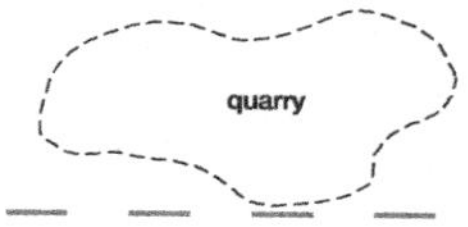

quarry

Craters

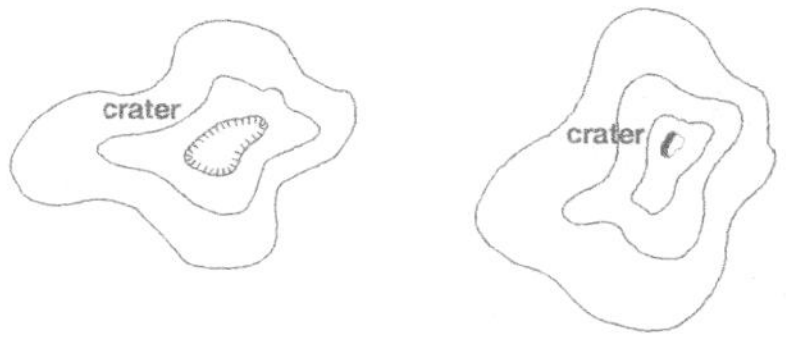

crater

crater

Unsurveyed Areas

Label appropriately as required

UNSURVEYED

Levees And Eskers

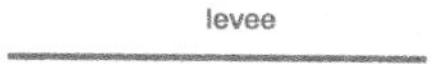

levee

Rock Strata Outcrop

rock strata

Strip Mines, Mine Dumps And Tailings

To Scale

strip mine   mine dump

Escarpments, Bluffs, Cliffs, Depressions, Etc.

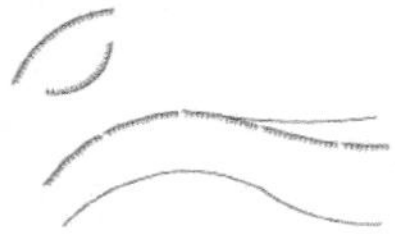

Uncontoured Areas

Label appropriately as required

RELIEF DATA INCOMPLETE

FAA Chart Users' Guide - VFR Symbology - Sectional and Terminal Area Charts

VFR FLYWAY PLANNING CHARTS

GENERAL INFORMATION

VFR Flyway Planning Charts are printed on the reverse sides of the Baltimore-Washington, Charlotte, Chicago, Cincinnati, Dallas-Ft. Worth, Denver, Detroit, Houston, Las Vegas, Los Angeles, Miami, Orlando, New Orleans, Phoenix, St. Louis, Salt Lake City, San Diego, San Francisco and Seattle Terminal Area Charts (TACs). The scale is 1:250,000, with area of coverage the same as the associated TACs. Flyway Planning Charts depict flight paths and altitudes recommended for use to by-pass areas heavily traversed by large turbine-powered aircraft. Ground references on these charts provide a guide for visual orientation. VFR Flyway Planning charts are designed for use in conjunction with TACs and are not to be used for navigation.

AIRPORTS

Landplane

No distinction is made between airports with fuel and those without fuel. Runways may be exaggerated to clearly portray the pattern. Hard-surfaced runways which are closed but still exist are included in the charted pattern.

FAR 91 - Fixed wing special VFR operations prohibited.

AGUA DOLCE (L7Ø)

Unpaved Runways

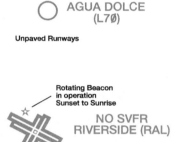

Rotating Beacon in operation Sunset to Sunrise

NO SVFR RIVERSIDE (RAL)

Paved Runways

Landplane (continued)

(Pvt): Non-public use having emergency or landmark value.

Ⓡ (Pvt) COMPTON

"OBJECTIONABLE": This airport may adversely affect airspace use.

◯ OBJECTIONABLE

ABANDONED - Depicted for landmark value or to prevent confusion with an adjacent usable landing area. Only portrayed beneath or close to the VFR flyway routes or requested by the FAA. (Normally at least 3000' paved).

⊗

RADIO AIDS TO NAVIGATION

VHF Omni-Directional Radio Range (VOR)

Identifier   Frequency

MAL 109.6

VORTAC

GCY 113.4

Crosshatch indicates Shutdown status

VOR-DME

FHM 114.2

Underline indicates no voice on this frequency

DME

PVU CH 21 (108.4)

Example: DME co-located at an airport.

DME
GVR CH 93 (114.65)

Non-Directional Radio Beacon (NDB)

WDP 396

Underline indicates no voice on this frequency

NDB-DME

LSJ 206

NAVAIDS Used to Define Class Airspace

ILS - DME

⊙ CLEVELAND-HOPKINS DME ANTENNA (I-HPI) Ch 36 (110.3)

Shared ILS - DME

⊙ MINNEAPOLIS DME ANTENNA (I-MSP/I-HKZ) Ch 40 (110.3)

AIRSPACE INFORMATION

FAA Chart Users' Guide - VFR Symbology - Flyway Planning Charts

Class B Airspace

Appropriate notes as required may be shown.

(Mode C see FAR 91.215/AIM)

All mileages are nautical (NM).

All radials are magnetic.

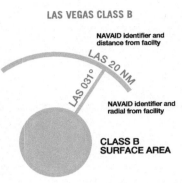

$\frac{80}{40}$ - Ceiling of Class B in hundreds of feet MSL
- Floor of Class B in hundreds of feet MSL

Floors extending "upward and above" a certain altitude are preceded by a +. Operations at or below these altitudes are outside of the Class B Airspace.)

Class D Airspace

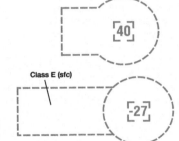

(A minus sign in front of the figure used to indicate "from surface to but not including...")

ALTITUDE IN HUNDREDS OF FEET MSL.

Class C Airspace

Appropriate notes as required may be shown.

(Mode C see FAR 91.215/AIM)

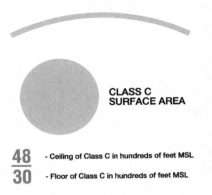

$\frac{48}{30}$ - Ceiling of Class C in hundreds of feet MSL
- Floor of Class C in hundreds of feet MSL

$\frac{T}{SFC}$ - Ceiling is to but not including floor of Class B
- Surface

Class E Surface (SFC) Airspace

Special Airspace Areas

Special Flight Rules Area (SFRA) Relating to National Security

Example: Washington DC

Appropriate notes as required may be shown.

Note: Delimiting line not shown when it coincides with International Boundary, projection lines or other linear features.

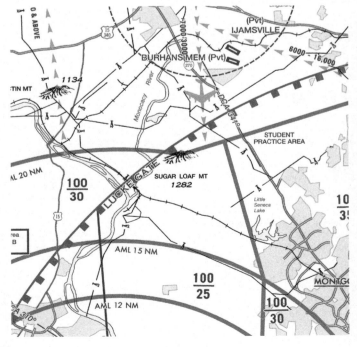

44

AIRSPACE INFORMATION (Continued)

Flight Restricted Zone (FRZ) Relating To National Security

Example: Washington DC

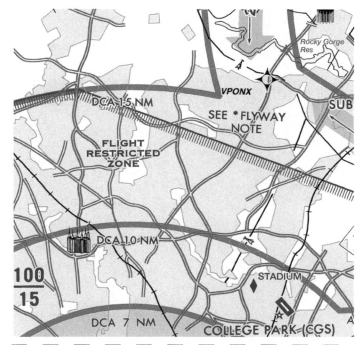

Temporary Flight Restriction (TFR) Relating To National Security

Example: Washington DC

Appropriate notes as required may be shown.

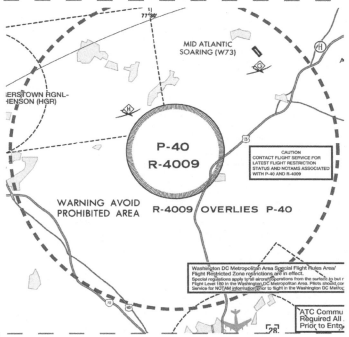

Special Use Airspace

Only the airspace effective below 18,000 feet MSL is shown.

The type of area shall be spelled out in large areas if space permits.

P-56 or R-6401 or W-518

PROHIBITED, RESTRICTED or WARNING AREA

FALCON 1 MOA or A-631

MILITARY OPERATIONS AREA (MOA) or ALERT AREA

Air Defense Identification Zone (ADIZ)

Note: Delimiting line not shown when it coincides with International Boundary, projection lines or other linear features.

CONTIGUOUS U.S. ADIZ

FAA Chart Users' Guide - VFR Chart Symbology - Flyway Planning Chars

AIRSPACE INFORMATION (Continued)

Special Air Traffic Rules/Airport Traffic Areas (FAR Part 93)

Appropriate boxed note as required shown adjacent to area. Inside the FAR Part 93 boundary area, the cross hatching is at a 45 degree angle.

Terminal Radar Service Area (TRSA)

TRSA SURFACE AREA

100 - Ceiling of TRSA in hundreds of feet MSL.
90 - Floor of TRSA in hundreds of feet MSL.

IFR Routes

Arrival

15,000 - 7000

Departure

8000 - 12,000

Arrival/Departure

IFR ARRIVALS   IFR DEPARTURES

8000 - 5000   5000 - 8000

VFR Transition Routes

Appropriate notes as required may be shown.

VFR TRANSITION ROUTE
ATC CLEARANCE REQUIRED
SEE SHOWBOAT GRAPHIC
ON SIDE PANEL

Uni-directional

Bi-directional

Bi-directional with NAVAID Ident and Radial

VNY 140°

Special Conservation Areas

NOAA Regulated National Marine Sanctuary Designated Areas

Flight operations below 1000' AGL over the designated areas within the Gulf of Farallones National Marine Sanctuary violate NOAA regulations (see 15 CFR 922).

Mode C (FAR 91.215)

Appropriate notes as required may be shown.

MODE C & ADS-B OUT
30 NM

Sporting Event Temporary Flight Restriction (TFR) Sites

STADIUM

National Defense Airspace Temporary Flight Restriction (TFR) Areas

Dallas National Defense Airspace TFR Check NOTAMs

Miscellaneous Activity Areas

Aerobatic Practice Area

Glider Operations

Hang Glider Activity

Ultralight Activity

Unmanned Aircraft Activity

Parachute Jumping Area with Frequency 122.9

Space Launch Activity Area

Example: Los Angeles

FAA Chart Users' Guide - VFR Symbology - Flyway Planning Charts

AIRSPACE INFORMATION (Continued)

Suggested VFR Flyway And Altitude

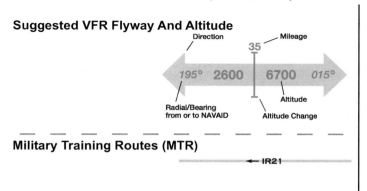

Military Training Routes (MTR)

← IR21

NAVIGATIONAL AND PROCEDURAL INFORMATION

VFR Checkpoints

Underline indicates proper name of VFR Checkpoint

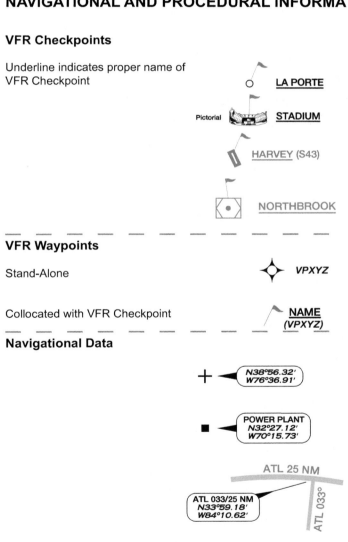

○ **LA PORTE**

Pictorial **STADIUM**

HARVEY (S43)

NORTHBROOK

VFR Waypoints

Stand-Alone

◆ *VPXYZ*

Collocated with VFR Checkpoint

NAME
(VPXYZ)

Navigational Data

+ ◀ N38°56.32'
W76°36.91'

■ ◀ POWER PLANT
N32°27.12'
W70°15.73'

ATL 25 NM

ATL 033/25 NM
N33°59.18'
W84°10.62'

ATL 033°

Obstructions

Only obstacles greater than 999' above ground level (AGL) or specified by the local ATC Facility shall be shown.

AGL heights are not shown. High-intensity lights may operate part-time or by proximity activation.

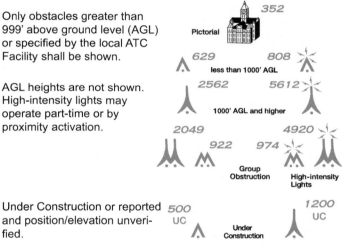

Pictorial 352

629 808
less than 1000' AGL

2562 5612
1000' AGL and higher

2049 4920
922 974
Group Obstruction   High-intensity Lights

Under Construction or reported and position/elevation unverified.

500 UC

1200 UC

Under Construction

FAA Chart Users' Guide - VFR Chart Symbology - Flyway Planning Chars

CULTURE

Railroads

Single and Multiple Tracks

Populated Places

Built-up Areas

BREMERTON

Towns ○ LAWRENCEVILLE

BOUNDARIES

International

HYDROGRAPHY

Shorelines

RELIEF

Spot Elevations
Position Accurate
Mountain Peaks

6504

Roads

Dual-Lane

HARBOR FREEWAY 110

Divided Highway Primary

40

Prominent Pictorials

TEMPLE

Power Transmission Lines

Landmarks

■ POWER PLANT

Reservoirs

Dam

Major Lakes and Rivers

Bridge

HELICOPTER ROUTE CHARTS

GENERAL INFORMATION

Helicopter Route Charts are three-color charts that depict current aeronautical information useful to helicopter pilots navigating in areas with high concentrations of helicopter activity. Information depicted includes helicopter routes, four classes of heliports with associated frequency and lighting capabilities, NAVAIDS, and obstructions. In addition, pictorial symbols, roads, and easily-identified geographical features are portrayed. The scale is 1:125,000. These charts are updated every three years or as needed to accommodate major changes.

AIRPORTS

Landplane

All recognizable runways, including some which may be closed, are shown for visual identification.

Public   ○

Private   ®

Unverified   Ⓤ

Abandoned   ⊗

Seaplane   ⚓

Airport Data Grouping

Boxed airport name indicates airport for which a Special Traffic Rule has been established.

(Pvt): Non-public use having emergency or landmark value. "OBJECTIONABLE": This airport may adversely affect airspace use.

Flight Service Station on field   FSS

Airspace where fixed wing special visual flight rules operations are prohibited (shown above airport name) FAR 91   NO SVFR

Indicates FAR 93 Special Air Traffic Rules and Airport Traffic   NAME

Location Idendtifier   (NAM)

ICAO Location Identifier   (PNAM)

Control Tower (CT) - primary frequency   CT - 119.1

Star indicates operation part-time. See tower frequencies tabulation for hours of operation   ★

When lighting is lacking, the respective character is replaced by a dash.

Heliport

Heliports public and private   Ⓗ

Medical Center   ⊕

Helipads located at major airports (when requested)   Ⓗ

Ultralight Flight Park   Ⓕ

```
          FSS
        NO SVFR
     NAME (NAM) (PNAM)
CT - 119.1 ★ Ⓒ (119.8 HELI)
       ATIS 115.4
    ASOS/AWOS 135.42
      285 L 122.95
       (Unverified)
          AOE
```

Automated Terminal Information Service   ATIS 115.4

Automated Surface Weather Observing Systems (shown when full-time ATIS is not available). Some ASOS/AWOS facilities may not be located at airports.   ASOS/AWOS 135.42

Elevation in feet   285

Lighting in operation Sunset to Sunshine   L

Lighting limitations exists, refer to Chart Supplement   *L

UNICOM - Aeronautical advisory station   122.95

Follows the Common Traffic Advisory Frequency (CTAF)   Ⓒ

Unverified Heliport   (Unverified)

Airport of Entry   AOE

Lighting codes refer to runway edge lights and may not represent the longest runway or full length lighting. Dashes are not shown on heliports or helipads unless additional information follows the elevation (e.g. UNICOM, CTAF).

FAA Chart Users' Guide - VFR Chart Symbology - Helicopter Charts

RADIO AIDS TO NAVIGATION

NAVAIDs

VHF Omni-Directional Radio (VOR) Range

Open circle symbol shown when NAVAID located on airport. Type of NAVAID shown in top of box.

Compass Rose is "reference" oriented to magnetic north.

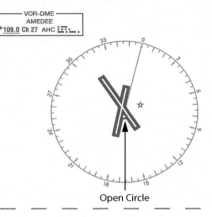

Open Circle

VOR

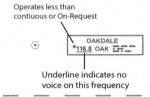

Operates less than contiuous or On-Request

Underline indicates no voice on this frequency

VORTAC

When an NDB NAVAID shares the same name and Morse Code as the VOR NAVAID the frequency can be collocated inside the same box to conserve space.

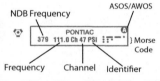

NDB Frequency

ASOS/AWOS

} Morse Code

Frequency   Channel   Identifier

VOR-DME

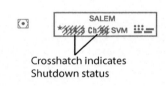

Crosshatch indicates Shutdown status

DME

Flight Service Station (FSS)

Heavy line box indicates Flight Service Station (FSS). Frequencies 122.2 and 255.4 (Conterminous U.S.); 121.5, 122.2, 243.0 and 255.4 (Alaska); and 121.5, 126.7, and 243.0 (Canada) are available at many FSSs and are not shown above boxes. All other frequencies are shown.

Certain FSSs provide Airport Advisory Service, refer to Chart Supplement.

R - Receive Only

DENVER DEN

122.1R   123.6
NORTHWAY
116.3 Ch 110 ORT

FSS oper 0600-2200
Rancho Murieta FSS other times.

123.6
ILIAMNA
411 ILI
DME Ch 91 (114.4)

Non-Directional Radio Beacon (NDB)

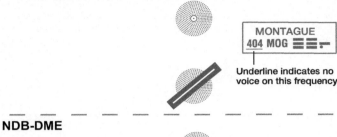

MONTAGUE
404 MOG

Underline indicates no voice on this frequency

NDB-DME

GAMBELL
369 GAM
DME Ch 92 (114.5)

NAVAID Used to Define Class B Airspace

ILS - DME
CLEVELAND-HOPKINS
DME ANTENNA
(I-HPI) Ch 36 (110.3)

Shared ILS - DME
MINNEAPOLIS
DME ANTENNA
(I-MSP/I-HKZ) Ch 40 (110.3)

Broadcast Stations (BS)

On request by the proper authority or when a VFR Checkpoint.

KFTM

BS
KFTM
1400

Remote Communications Outlet (RCO)

Frequencies above thin line box are remoted to NAVAID site. Other FSS frequencies providing voice communications may be available as determined by altitude and terrain. Consult Chart Supplement for complete information.

Thin line box without frequencies and controlling FSS name indicates no FSS frequency available.

123.6
OLYMPIA RCO
MCCHORD

122.1R
FREDERICK
109.9 FDK
LEESBURG

122.25
TOGIAK
393 TOG
DME Ch 114 (116.7)
KENAI

AIRSPACE INFORMATION

Class B Airspace

Appropriate notes as required may be shown. (Mode C see FAR 91.215/AIM)

All mileages are nautical (NM)

(Floors extending "upward from above" a certain altitude are preceded by a +. Operations at and below these altitudes are outside of Class B Airspace.)

All radials are magnetic.

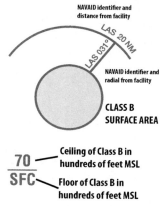

CTC LAS VEGAS APP ON 121.1 OR 257.8

Class C Airspace

Appropriate notes as required may be shown. (Mode C see FAR 91.215/AIM)

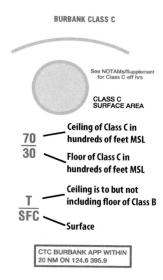

CTC BURBANK APP WITHIN 20 NM ON 124.6 395.9

Class D Airspace

(A minus in front of the figure is used to indicate "from surface to but not including...")

Altitudes in hundreds of feet MSL.

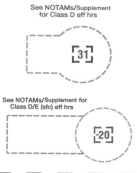

Class E Surface (SFC) Airspace

See NOTAMs/Supplement for Class E (sfc) eff hrs

Special Airspace Areas

Special Flight Rules Area (SFRA) Relating to National Security

Example: Washington DC

Appropriate notes as required may be shown.

Note: Delimiting line not shown when it coincides with International Boundary, projection lines or other linear features.

WASHINGTON DC METROPOLITAN AREA SFRA

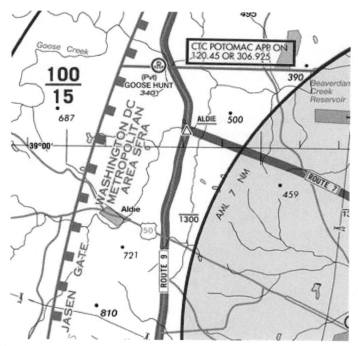

FAA Chart Users' Guide - VFR Chart Symbology - Helicopter Charts

AIRSPACE INFORMATION (Continued)

Special Airspace Areas (Continued)

Flight Restricted Zone (FRZ) Relating to National Security

Example: Washington DC

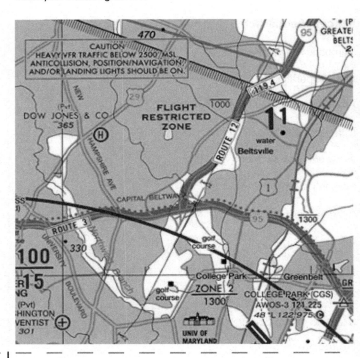

Air Defense Identification Zone (ADIZ)

Note: Delimiting line not shown when it coincides with International Boundary, projection lines or other linear features.

CONTIGUOUS
U.S. ADIZ

Special Security Notice Permanent Continuous Flight Restriction Areas

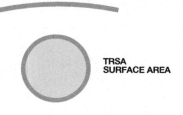

DISNEYLAND THEME PARK
See Panel for requirements

Mode C (FAR 91.215)

Appropriate notes as required may be shown.

MODE C & ADS-B OUT
30 NM

Terminal Radar Service Area (TRSA)

PALM SPRINGS TRSA

Appropriate notes as required may be shown.

TRSA
SURFACE AREA

SEE TWR FREQ TAB

$\frac{80}{40}$ - Ceiling of TRSA in hundreds of feet MSL
- Floor of TRSA in hundreds of feet MSL

Special Air Traffic Rules / Airport Traffic Areas (FAR Part 93)

Appropriate boxed notes as required shown adjacent to area. Inside the FAR Part 93 boundary area, the cross hatching is at a 45 degree angle.

SPECIAL NOTICE
Pilots are required to obtain an ATC clearance prior to entering this area.

Sporting Event Temporary Flight Restriction (TFR) Sites

◆ STADIUM

National Defense Airspace Temporary Flight Restriction (TFR) Areas

Dallas National
Defense Airspace TFR
Check NOTAMs

AIRSPACE INFORMATION (Continued)

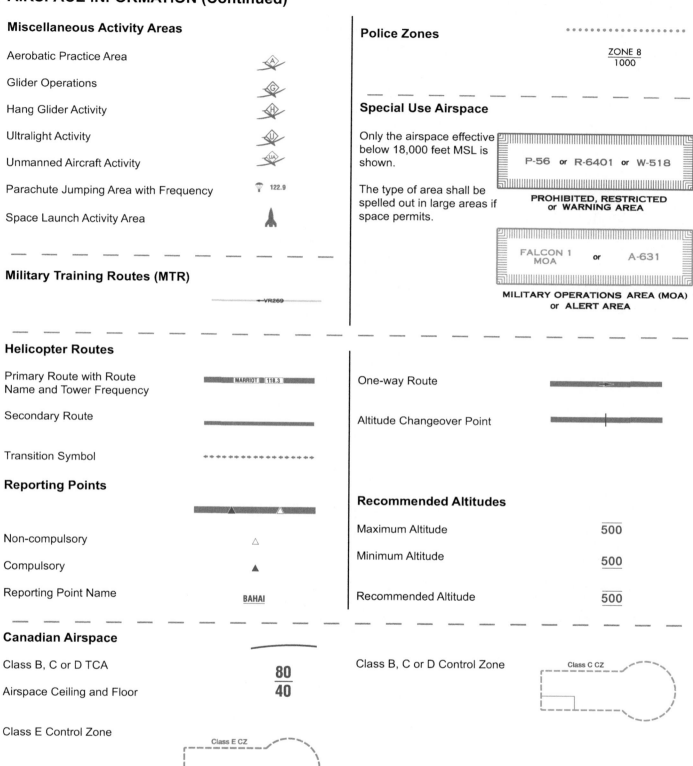

Miscellaneous Activity Areas

Aerobatic Practice Area

Glider Operations

Hang Glider Activity

Ultralight Activity

Unmanned Aircraft Activity

Parachute Jumping Area with Frequency   122.9

Space Launch Activity Area

Military Training Routes (MTR)

VR269

Helicopter Routes

Primary Route with Route Name and Tower Frequency   MARRIOT 118.3

Secondary Route

Transition Symbol

Reporting Points

Non-compulsory   △

Compulsory   ▲

Reporting Point Name   BAHAI

Canadian Airspace

Class B, C or D TCA

Airspace Ceiling and Floor $\frac{80}{40}$

Class E Control Zone

Class E CZ

Police Zones

ZONE 8
1000

Special Use Airspace

Only the airspace effective below 18,000 feet MSL is shown.

The type of area shall be spelled out in large areas if space permits.

P-56   or   R-6401   or   W-518

PROHIBITED, RESTRICTED or WARNING AREA

FALCON 1 MOA   or   A-631

MILITARY OPERATIONS AREA (MOA) or ALERT AREA

One-way Route

Altitude Changeover Point

Recommended Altitudes

Maximum Altitude   500

Minimum Altitude   500

Recommended Altitude   500

Class B, C or D Control Zone   Class C CZ

FAA Chart Users' Guide - VFR Chart Symbology - Helicopter Charts

AIRSPACE INFORMATION (Continued)

FAA Chart Users' Guide - VFR Chart Symbology - Helicopter Charts

Special Conservation Areas

National Park, Wildlife Refuge, Primitive and Wilderness Areas, etc.

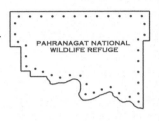

NOAA Regulated National Marine Sanctuary Designated Areas

Flight operations below 1000' AGL over the designated areas within the Gulf of Farallones National Marine Sanctuary violate NOAA regulations (see 15 CFR 922).

NAVIGATIONAL AND PROCEDURAL INFORMATION

VFR Checkpoints

Underline indicates proper name of VFR Checkpoint.

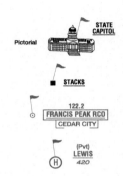

VFR Waypoints

Stand-Alone

 VPXYZ

Collocated with VFR Checkpoint

 NAME *(VPXYZ)*

Collocated with VFR Checkpoint & Reporting Point

 NAME *(VPXYZ)*

Obstruction

Above 299' and below 1000' AGL

1000' and higher AGL

Group Obstruction

Above 299' and below 1000' AGL

1000' and higher AGL

High-Intensity Obstruction Lights

High-intensity lights may operate part-time or by proximity activation.

Wind Turbine Farms

When highest wind turbine is unverified, UC will be shown after MSL value.

Navigation Data

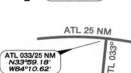

Maximum Elevation Figure (MEF)

(see VFR Terms tab for explanation)

124

CULTURE

Railroads

Single Track

Double Track

Bridges

Railroad

Road

Populated Places

Built-up Areas

Roads

HOLLYWOOD BOULEVARD

Dual-Lane:
Divided Highways

(495)

Major Boulevards & Major Streets
Primary

(95)

(25)

Boundaries

International

State or Province

Power Transmission Lines

Prominent Pictorials

TEMPLE

Landmarks

■ Landmark-stadium, factory, school, etc.

▲ Lookout Tower

⚒ Mines or Quarries

⊜ Race Track

♒ Outdoor Theater

● Tank-water, oil or gas

FAA Chart Users' Guide - VFR Chart Symbology - Helicopter Charts

AIRSPACE

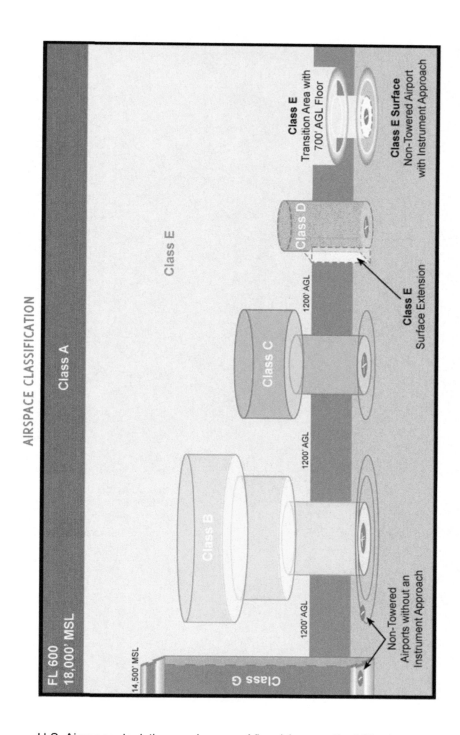

U.S. Airspace depiction as shown on Visual Aeronautical Charts

57

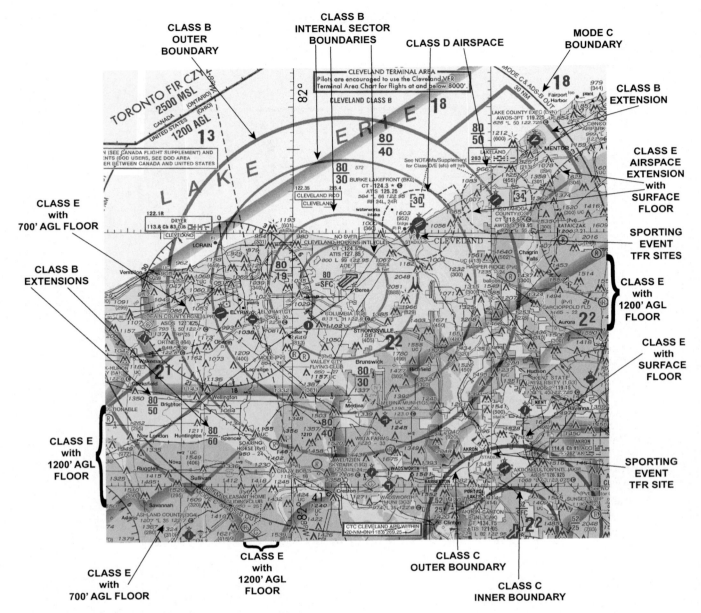

Excerpt from Detroit Sectional Chart

EXPLANATION OF IFR ENROUTE TERMS

FAA charts are prepared in accordance with specifications of the Interagency Air Committee (IAC), and are approved by representatives of the Federal Aviation Administration and the Department of Defense (DoD). Some information on these charts may only apply to military pilots.

The explanations of symbols used on Instrument Flight Rule (IFR) Enroute Charts and examples in this section are based primarily on the IFR Enroute Low Altitude Charts. Other IFR products use similar symbols in various colors. The chart legends portray aeronautical symbols with a brief description of what each symbol depicts. This section provides more details of the symbols and how they are used on IFR Enroute charts.

AIRPORTS

Operational airports are shown on IFR Enroute Charts.

Low Charts:

- All IAP Airports are shown on the Low Altitude Charts (US and Alaska).

- Non-IAP Airports are shown on the U.S. Low Altitude Charts (Contiguous US) have a minimum hard surface runway of 3,000'.

- Non-IAP airports are shown on the U.S. Low Altitude Alaska Charts are show if the runway is 3000' or longer, hard or soft surface.

- Public heliports with an Instrument Approach Procedure (IAP) or requested by the FAA or DoD are depicted on the IFR Enroute Low Altitude Charts.

- Seaplane bases requested by the FAA or DoD are depicted on the IFR Enroute Low Altitude Charts.

On IFR Enroute Low Altitude Charts, airport tabulation is provided which identifies airport names, IDs and the panels they are located on.

High Charts:

- Airports shown on the U.S. High Enroute Charts (Contiguous US) have a minimum hard surface runway of 5000'.

- Airports shown on the U.S. High Enroute Alaska Charts have a minimum hard surface runway of 4000'.

Charted airports are classified according to the following criteria:

LOW/HIGH ALTITUDE

Blue - Airports with an Instrument Approach Procedure and/or RADAR MINIMA published in the high altitude DoD Flight Information Publications (FLIPs)

Green - Airports which have an approved Instrument Approach Procedure and/or RADAR MINIMA published in either the U.S. Terminal Procedures Publications (TPPs) or the DoD FLIPs

Brown - Airports without a published Instrument Approach Procedure or RADAR MINIMA

Airports are plotted at their true geographic position.

Airports are identified by the airport name. In the case of military airports, Air Force Base (AFB), Naval Air Station (NAS), Naval Air Facility (NAF), Marine Corps Air Station (MCAS), Army Air Field (AAF), etc., the abbreviated letters appear as part of the airport name.

Airports marked "Pvt" immediately following the airport name are not for public use, but otherwise meet the criteria for charting as specified above.

Runway length is the length of the longest active runway (including displaced thresholds but excluding overruns) and is shown to the nearest 100 feet using 70 feet as the division point; e.g., a runway of 8,070' is labeled 81. The following runway compositions (materials) constitute a hard-surfaced runway: asphalt, bitumen, chip seal, concrete, and tar macadam. Runways that are not hard-surfaced have a small letter "s" following the runway length, indicating a soft surface.

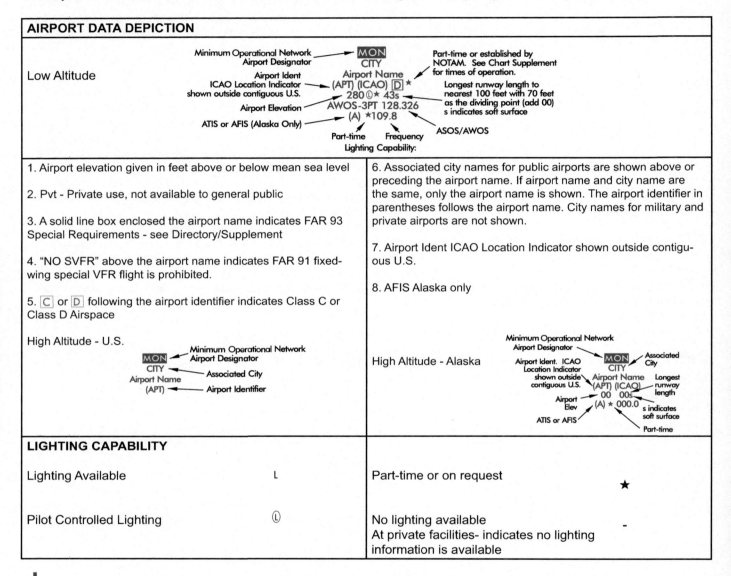

AIRPORT DATA DEPICTION

1. Airport elevation given in feet above or below mean sea level

2. Pvt - Private use, not available to general public

3. A solid line box enclosed the airport name indicates FAR 93 Special Requirements - see Directory/Supplement

4. "NO SVFR" above the airport name indicates FAR 91 fixed-wing special VFR flight is prohibited.

5. C or D following the airport identifier indicates Class C or Class D Airspace

6. Associated city names for public airports are shown above or preceding the airport name. If airport name and city name are the same, only the airport name is shown. The airport identifier in parentheses follows the airport name. City names for military and private airports are not shown.

7. Airport Ident ICAO Location Indicator shown outside contiguous U.S.

8. AFIS Alaska only

LIGHTING CAPABILITY

Lighting Available	L
Pilot Controlled Lighting	Ⓛ
Part-time or on request	★
No lighting available	-
At private facilities- indicates no lighting information is available	

A L symbol between the airport elevation and runway length means that runway lights are in operation sunset to sunrise.

A Ⓛ symbol indicates there is Pilot Controlled Lighting. A L★ symbol means the lighting is part-time or on request, the pilot should consult the Chart Supplement for light operating procedures. The Aeronautical Information Manual (AIM) thoroughly explains the types and uses of airport lighting aids.

VOR Minimum Operational Network (MON) Airports Designator

MON Airports with the MON Airport designator at the top of the Airport Data Block. The MON designation is to alert pilots to those airports that have retained ILS and VOR instrument approach procedures for safe recovery in the event of a GPS outage. Refer to the Aeronautical Information Manual (AIM) for expanded MON Airport guidance.

RADIO AIDS TO NAVIGATION

All IFR radio NAVAIDs that have been flight checked and are operational are shown on all IFR Enroute Charts. Very High Frequency/Ultrahigh Frequency (VHF/UHF) NAVAIDs, Very high frequency Omnidirectional Radio range (VORs), Tactical Air Navigation (TACANs) are shown in black, and Low Frequency/Medium Frequency (LF/MF) NAVAIDs, (Compass Locators and Aeronautical or Marine NDBs) are shown in brown.

On IFR Enroute Charts, information about NAVAIDs is boxed as illustrated below. To avoid duplication of data, when two or more NAVAIDs in a general area have the same name, the name is usually printed only once inside an identification box with the frequencies, TACAN channel numbers, identification letters, or Morse Code Identifications of the different NAVAIDs are shown in appropriate colors.

NAVAIDs in a shutdown status have the frequency and channel number crosshatched. Use of the NAVAID status "shutdown" is only used when a facility has been decommissioned but cannot be published as such because of pending airspace actions.

NAVIGATION AND COMMUNICATION BOXES - COMMON ELEMENTS	
LOW ENROUTE CHARTS	**HIGH ENROUTE CHARTS**
RCO Frequencies 000.0 NAVAID Name, SSV(s) NAME (VL) (T) FREQ, Ident, CH, Morse Code 000.0 IDT 000 ≝·· Latitude, Longitude N00°00.00′ W000°00.00′ Controlling FSS Name ⌊NAME⌋	RCO Frequencies 000.0 NAVAID Name NAME Frequency, Ident, SSV(s), Channel 000.0 IDT (H) (DL) 000 Latitude, Longitude N00°00.00′ W000°00.00′ Controlling FSS Name ⌊NAME⌋
COMMON ELEMENTS (HIGH AND LOW CHARTS)	
RCO FREQUENCY Single Frequency Multiple Frequencies Frequencies transmit and receive except those followed by R and T: R - Receive Only T - Transmit Only	122.6 255.4 243.0 123.6 122.65 122.2 122.1R 121.5
NAVAID BOX Thin line NAVAID boxes without frequency(s) and FSS radio name indicates no FSS frequencies available. Shadow NAVAID box indicates NAVAID and Flight Service Station (FSS) have same name.	VHF/UHF LF/MF

FAA Chart Users' Guide - IFR Enroute Terms

NAVAID STANDARD SERVICE VOLUME (SSV) CLASSIFICATIONS

SSV Class	Altitudes	Distance (NM)
(T) Terminal	1000' to 12,000'	25
(L) Low Altitude	1000' to 18,000'	40
(H) High Altitude	1000' to 14,500' 14,500' to 18,000' 18,000' to 45,000' 45,000' to 60,000'	40 100 130 100
(VL) VOR Low	1000' to 5,000' 5,000' to 18,000'	40 70
(VH) VOR High	1000' to 5,000' 5,000' to 14,500' 14,500' to 18,000' 18,000' to 45,000' 45,000' to 60,000'	40 70 100 130 100
(DL) DME Low & (DH) DME High*	1000' to 12,900'	40 increasing to 130
(DL) DME Low	12,900' to 18,000'	130
(DH) DME High	12,900' to 45,000' 45,000' to 60,000'	130 100

* Between 1000' to 12,900', DME service volume follows a parabolic curve used by flight managment computers.

Notes: Additionally, High Altitude facilities provide Low Altitude and Terminal service volume and Low Altitude facilities provide Terminal service volume. Altitudes are with respect to the station's site elevation. Coverage is not available in a cone of airspace directly above the facility. In some cases local conditions (terrain, buildings, trees, etc.) may require that the service volume be restricted. The public shall be informed of any such restriction by a remark in the NAVAID entry or by a Notice to Air Missions (NOTAM).

DISTANCE MEASURING EQUIPMENT *Facilities that operate in the "Y" mode for DME reception*	(Y)
VOICE COMMUNICATIONS VIA NAVAID *Voice Transmitted* *No Voice Transmitted*	 112.6 111.0

NAVAID SHUTDOWN STATUS	**VHF/UHF** **LF/MF**

PART TIME OR ON-REQUEST	**VHF/UHF** **LF/MF** ★ ★

AUTOMATED WEATHER BROADCAST SERVICES **ASOS/AWOS** - *Automated Surface Observing Station/Automated Weather Observing Station*	VHF/UHF LF/MF Ⓐ Ⓐ *Automated weather, when available, is broadcast on the associated NAVAID frequency.*

LATITUDE AND LONGITUDE *Latitude and Longitude coordinates are provided for those NAVAIDs that make up part of a route/airway or a holding pattern. All TACAN facilities will include geographic coordinates.*	**LOW ENROUTE** **HIGH ENROUTE** *N00°00.00' W000°00.00'* *N00°00.00'* *W000°00.00'*

AIRSPACE INFORMATION

CONTROLLED AIRSPACE

Controlled airspace consists of those areas where some or all aircraft are subjected to air traffic control within the following airspace classifications of A, B, C, D, & E.

Air Route Traffic Control Centers (ARTCC) are established to provide Air Traffic Control to aircraft operating on IFR flight plans within controlled airspace, particularly during the enroute phase of flight. Boundaries of the ARTCCs are shown in their entirety using the symbol below.

Air Route Traffic Control Center (ARTCC)

When Controller Pilot Data Link Communication (CPDLC) exists for an ARTCC, the text CPDLC (LOGON KUSA) will be shown parallel to the boundary above or below the ARTCC identification as shown below.

ATLANTA
JACKSONVILLE
CPDLC (LOGON KUSA)

CPDLC (LOGON KUSA)
ATLANTA
JACKSONVILLE
CPDLC (LOGON KUSA)

Air Route Traffic Control Center (ARTCC) with
Controller Pilot Data Link Communication (CPDLC)

The responsible ARTCC Center names are shown adjacent and parallel to the boundary line. ARTCC sector frequencies are shown in boxes outlined by the same symbol.

NEW YORK — ARTCC Name
Barnegat — Site Name
132.15 — Frequency

ARTCC Remoted Sites with
discrete VHF and UHF frequencies

Class A Airspace is depicted as open area (white) on the IFR Enroute High Altitude Charts. It consists of airspace from 18,000 Mean Sea Level (MSL) to FL600.

Class B Airspace is depicted as screened blue area with a solid line encompassing the area.

Class C Airspace is depicted as screened blue area with a dashed line encompassing the area with a letter "C" enclosed in a box following the airport name.

Class B and Class C Airspace consist of controlled airspace extending upward from the surface or a designated floor to specified altitudes, within which all aircraft and pilots are subject to the operating rules and requirements specified in the Federal Aviation Regulations (UHF) 71. Class B and C Airspace are shown in abbreviated forms on IFR Enroute Low Altitude Charts. A general note adjacent to Class B airspace refers the user to the appropriate VFR Terminal Area Chart.

Class D Airspace (airports with an operating control tower) are depicted as open area (white) with a letter "D" enclosed in a box following the airport name.

Class E Airspace is depicted as open area (white) on the IFR Enroute Low Altitude Charts. It consists of airspace below FL180.

UNCONTROLLED AIRSPACE

Class G Airspace within the United States extends to 14,500' MSL. This uncontrolled airspace is shown as screened brown.

SPECIAL USE AIRSPACE

Special Use Airspace (SUA) confines certain flight activities, restricts entry, or cautions other aircraft operating within specific boundaries. SUA areas are shown in their entirety, even when they overlap, adjoin, or when an area is designated within another area. SUA with altitudes from the surface and above are shown on the IFR Enroute Low Altitude Charts. Similarly, SUA that extends above 18,000' MSL are shown on IFR Enroute High Altitude Charts. IFR Enroute Charts tabulations identify the type of SUA, ID, effective altitudes, times of use, controlling agency and the panel it is located on.

Users need to be aware that a NOTAM addressing activation will NOT be issued to announce permanently listed times of use.

| P-56 |
| R-123 |
| W-789 |
| CYA-101 |
| CYD-102 |
| CYR-103 |

| A-456 |

| WALL 1 MOA |
| WALL 2 MOA |

Line delimits internal separation of same Special Use Area

High and Low	Low Altitude Only	Canada Only	Caribbean Only
P - Prohibited Area	MOA - Military Operations Area	CYA - Advisory	D - Danger
R - Restricted Area	A - Alert Area *	CYD - Danger Area	
W - Warning Area		CYR - Restricted Area	
* Alert Areas do not extend into Class A, B, C and D airspace, or Class E airport surface areas.			
See Airspace Tabulation on chart for complete information.			

OTHER AIRSPACE

FAR 91 Special Air Traffic Rules are shown with the type NO SVFR above the airport name.

NO SVFR
Baltimore/Washington Intl
Thurgood Marshall
(BWI)
143 L 105
(A) 115.1 127.8

FAR 93 Special Airspace Traffic Rules are shown with a solid line box around the airport name, indicating FAR 93 Special Requirements see Chart Supplement.

NO SVFR
NEW YORK
John F Kennedy Intl
(JFK)
13 L 145
(A) ARR 115.4 SW 117.7 NE
ARR/DEP 128.725

Mode C Required Airspace (from the surface to 10,000' MSL) within 30 NM radius of the primary airport(s) for which a Class B airspace is designated, is depicted on IFR Enroute Low Altitude Charts as a blue circle labeled MODE C & ADS-B OUT 30 NM.

Mode C & ADS-B Out is also required for operations within and above all Class C airspace up to 10,000' MSL, but not depicted. See FAR 91.215 and the AIM.

INSTRUMENT AIRWAYS

The FAA has established two fixed route systems for air navigation. The VOR and LF/MF system-designated from 1,200' Above Ground Level (AGL) to but not including FL 180 is shown on IFR Enroute Low Altitude Charts, and the Jet Route system designated from FL 180 to FL 450 inclusive is shown on IFR Enroute High Altitude Charts.

VOR LF/MF AIRWAY SYSTEM (IFR LOW ALTITUDE ENROUTE CHARTS)

In this system VOR airways - airways based on VOR or VORTAC NAVAIDs - are depicted in black and identified by a "V" (Victor) followed by the route number (e.g., "V12").

LF/MF airways - airways based on LF/MF NAVAIDs - are sometimes called "colored airways" because they are identified by color name and number (e.g., "Amber One", charted as "A1"). In Alaska Green and Red airways are plotted east and west, and Amber and Blue airways are plotted north and south. Regardless of their color identifier, LF/MF airways are shown in brown.

AIRWAY/ROUTE DATA

On both series of IFR Enroute Charts, airway/route data such as the airway identifications, magnetic courses bearings or radials, mileages, and altitudes (e.g., Minimum Enroute Altitudes (MEAs), Minimum Reception Altitudes (MRAs), Maximum Authorized Altitudes (MAAs), Minimum Obstacle Clearance Altitudes (MOCAs), Minimum Turning Altitudes (MTAs) and Minimum Crossing Altitudes (MCAs)) are shown aligned with the airway.

As a rule the airway/route data is charted and in the same color as the airway, with one exception. Charted in blue, Global Navigation Satellite System (GNSS) MEAs, identified with a "G" suffix, have been added to "V" and "colored airways" for aircraft flying those airways using Global Positioning System (GPS) navigation.

Airways/Routes predicated on VOR or VORTAC NAVAIDs are defined by the outbound radial from the NAVAID. Airways/Routes predicated on LF/MF NAVAIDs are defined by the inbound bearing.

- **Minimum Enroute Altitude (MEA)** - The MEA is the lowest published altitude between radio fixes that assures acceptable navigational signal coverage and meets obstacle clearance requirements between those fixes. The MEA prescribed for a Federal airway or segment, RNAV low or high route, or other direct route applies to the entire width of the airway, segment, or route between the radio fixes defining the airway, segment, or route. MEAs for routes wholly contained within controlled airspace normally provide a buffer above the floor of controlled airspace consisting of at least 300 feet within transition areas and 500 feet within control areas. MEAs are established based upon obstacle clearance over terrain and man-made objects, adequacy of navigation facility performance, and communications requirements.

- **Minimum Reception Altitude (MRA)** - MRAs are determined by FAA flight inspection traversing an entire route of flight to establish the minimum altitude the navigation signal can be received for the route and for off-course NAVAID facilities that determine a fix. When the MRA at the fix is higher than the MEA, an MRA is established for the fix and is the lowest altitude at which an intersection can be determined.

- **Maximum Authorized Altitude (MAA)** - An MAA is a published altitude representing the maximum usable altitude or flight level for an airspace structure or route segment. It is the highest altitude on a Federal airway, jet route, RNAV low or high route, or other direct route for which an MEA is designated at which adequate reception of navigation signals is assured.

- **Minimum Obstruction Clearance Altitude (MOCA)** - The MOCA is the lowest published altitude in effect between radio fixes on VOR airways, off-airway routes, or route segments which meets obstacle clearance requirements for the entire route segment and which assures acceptable navigational signal coverage only within 25 statute (22 nautical) miles of a VOR. A MOCA is only shown on the Enroute Low Charts and only published when it is lower than the MEA. When shown, it is preceded by an asterisk.

- **Minimum Turning Altitude (MTA)** - Minimum turning altitude (MTA) is a charted altitude providing vertical and lateral obstruction clearance based on turn criteria over certain fixes, NAVAIDs, waypoints, and on charted route segments. When a VHF airway or route terminates at a NAVAID or fix, the primary area extends beyond that termination point. When a change of course on VHF airways and routes is necessary, the enroute obstacle clearance turning area extends the primary and secondary obstacle clearance areas to accommodate the turn radius of the aircraft. Since turns at or after fix passage may exceed airway and route boundaries, pilots are expected to adhere to airway and route protected airspace by leading turns early before a fix. The turn area provides obstacle clearance for both turn anticipation (turning prior to the fix) and flyover protection (turning after crossing the fix). Turning fixes requiring a higher MTA are charted with a flag along with accompanying text describing the MTA restriction.

- **Minimum Crossing Altitude (MCA)** - An MCA is the lowest altitude at certain fixes at which the aircraft must cross when proceeding in the direction of a higher minimum enroute IFR altitude. MCAs are established in all cases where obstacles intervene to prevent pilots from maintaining obstacle clearance during a normal climb to a higher MEA after passing a point beyond which the higher MEA applies. The same protected enroute area vertical obstacle clearance requirements for the primary and secondary areas are considered in the determination of the MCA.

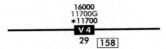

Victor Route (with RNAV/GPS MEA shown in blue)

AREA NAVIGATION (RNAV) "T" ROUTE SYSTEM

The FAA has created new low altitude area navigation (RNAV) "T" routes for the enroute and terminal environments. The RNAV routes will provide more direct routing for IFR aircraft and enhance the safety and efficiency of the National Airspace System. To utilize these routes aircraft are required to be equipped with IFR approved GNSS. In Alaska, TSO-145a and 146a equipment is required.

Low altitude RNAV only routes are identified by the prefix "T", and the prefix "TK" for RNAV helicopter routes followed by a three digit number (T-200 to T-500). Routes are depicted in blue on the IFR Enroute Low Altitude Charts. RNAV route data (route line, identification boxes, mileages, waypoints, waypoint names, magnetic reference courses and MEAs) will also be printed in blue. Magnetic reference courses will be shown originating from a waypoint, fix/reporting point or NAVAID. GNSS MEA for each segment is established to ensure obstacle clearance and communications reception. GNSS MEAs are identified with a "G" suffix.

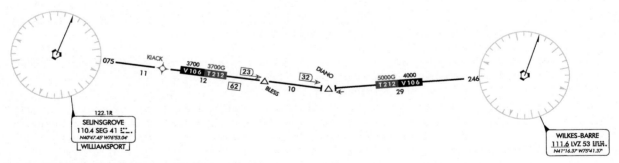

Joint Victor/RNAV routes are charted as outlined above except as noted. The joint Victor route and the RNAV route identification boxes are shown adjacent to each other. Magnetic reference courses are not shown. MEAs are charted above the appropriate identification box or stacked in pairs, GNSS and Victor. On joint routes, RNAV specific information will be printed in blue.

UNUSABLE AIRWAY/ROUTE SEGMENTS

Airway/Route segments designated by the FAA as unusable will be depicted as shown below.

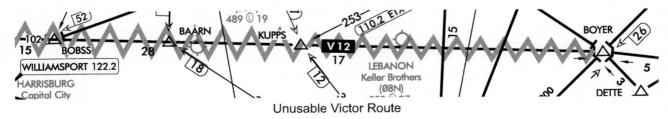

Unusable Victor Route

Pilots should not file a flight plan for or accept a clearance that includes navigation on any route or route segment depicted as unusable. Pilots using RNAV may request ATC clearance to fly point-to-point between valid waypoints or fixes, even those on routes depicted as unusable (refer to AC 90-108 for RNAV eligibility).

Coincident Airways/Routes with Unusable Segment

When two airways/routes are coincident, but only one airway/route is designated as unusable, the following note indicating which airway the unusable symbology applies to will be placed in close proximity to the airway/route identifiers.

ONLY J91 UNUSABLE

OFF ROUTE OBSTRUCTION CLEARANCE ALTITUDE (OROCA)

The Off Route Obstruction Clearance Altitude (OROCA) is depicted on IFR Enroute Low Altitude and Pacific charts and is represented in thousands and hundreds of feet above MSL. OROCAs are shown in every 30 x 30 minute quadrant on Area Charts, every one degree by one degree quadrant for IFR Enroute Low Altitude Charts - U.S. and every two de¬gree by two degree quadrant on IFR Enroute Low Altitude Charts - Alaska. The OROCA is based on the highest known terrain feature or obstruction in each quadrangle, bounded by the ticked lines of latitude/longitude including data 4 NM outside the quadrant. In this example the OROCA represents 12,500 feet.

OROCA is computed just as the Maximum Elevation Figure (MEF) found on Visual Flight Rule (VFR) Charts except that it provides an additional vertical buffer of 1,000 feet in designated non-mountainous areas and a 2,000 foot vertical buffer in designated mountainous areas within the United States. For areas in Mexico and the Caribbean, located outside the U.S. Air Defense Identification Zone (ADIZ), the OROCA provides obstruction clearance with a 3,000 foot vertical buffer. Evaluating the area around the quadrant provides the chart user the same lateral clearance an airway provides should the line of intended flight follow a ticked line of latitude or longitude. OROCA altitudes are not assessed for NAVAID signal coverage, air traffic control surveillance, or communications coverage, and are published for general situational awareness, flight planning, and in-flight contingency use. OROCAs can be found over all land masses and open water areas containing man-made obstructions (such as oil rigs).

$$12^5$$

MILITARY TRAINING ROUTES (MTRs)

Military Training Routes (MTRs) are routes established for the conduct of low-altitude, high-speed military flight training (generally below 10,000 feet MSL at airspeeds in excess of 250 knots Indicated Air Speed). These routes are depicted in brown on IFR Enroute Low Altitude Charts, and are not shown on inset charts or on IFR Enroute High Altitude Charts. IFR Enroute Low Altitude Charts depict all IFR Military Training Routes (IRs) and VFR Military Training Routes (VRs), except those VRs that are entirely at or below 1,500 feet AGL.

MTRs are identified by designators (IR-107, VR-134) which are shown in brown on the route centerline. Arrows are shown to indicate the direction of flight along the route. The width of the route determines the width of the line that is plotted on the chart:

Route segments with a width of 5 NM or less, both sides of the centerline, are shown by a .02" line.

———— IR 000 → ————

Route segments with a width greater than 5 NM, either or both sides of the centerline, are shown by a .035" line.

———— VR 000 → ————

MTRs for particular chart pairs (ex. L1/2, etc.) are alphabetically, then numerically tabulated. The tabulation includes MTR type and unique identification and altitude range.

JET ROUTE SYSTEM (HIGH ALTITUDE ENROUTE CHARTS)

Jet routes are based on VOR or VORTAC NAVAIDs, and are depicted in black with a "J" identifier followed by the route number (e.g., "J12"). In Alaska, Russia and Canada some segments of jet routes are based on LF/MF NAVAIDs.

AREA NAVIGATION (RNAV) "Q" ROUTE SYSTEM (IFR ENROUTE HIGH ALTITUDE CHARTS)

The FAA has adopted certain amendments to Title 14, Code of Federal Regulations which paved the way for the development of new area high altitude navigation (RNAV) "Q" routes in the U.S. National Airspace System (NAS). These amendments enable the FAA to take advantage of technological advancements in navigation systems such as the GPS. RNAV "Q" Route MEAs are shown when other than FL 180 MEAs for DME/DME/Inertial Reference Unit (IRU) RNAV aircraft have a "D" suffix.

RNAV routes and associated data are charted in blue. "Q" Routes on the IFR Gulf of Mexico charts are shown in black. Magnetic reference courses are shown originating from a waypoint, fix/reporting point, or NAVAID.

Joint Jet/RNAV route identification boxes will be located adjacent to each other with the route charted in black. With the exception of Q-Routes in the Gulf of Mexico, GNSS or DME/DME/IRU RNAV are required, unless otherwise indicated. Q-Routes in Alaska are GNSS Only. Altitude values are stacked highest to lowest.

J45 Q19
95
Joint Jet/RNAV Route

TERRAIN CONTOURS ON AREA CHARTS

Based on a recommendation of the National Transportation Safety Board, terrain contours have been added to the Enroute Area Charts and are intended to increase pilots' situational awareness for safe flight over changes in terrain. The following Area Charts portray terrain: Anchorage, Denver, Fairbanks, Juneau, Los Angeles, Nome, Phoenix, San Francisco, Vancouver and Washington.

When terrain rises at least a 1,000 feet above the primary airports' elevation, terrain is charted using shades of brown with brown contour lines and values. The initial contour will be 1,000 or 2,000 feet above the airports' elevation. Subsequent intervals will be 2,000 or 3,000 foot increments.

Contours are supplemented with a representative number of spots elevations and are shown in solid black. The highest elevation on an Area Chart is shown with a larger spot and text.

The following boxed note is added to the affected Area Charts.

NOTE: TERRAIN CONTOURS HAVE BEEN ADDED TO THOSE AREA CHARTS WHERE THE TERRAIN ON THE CHART IS 1000 FOOT OR GREATER THAN THE ELEVATION OF THE PRIMARY AIRPORT

IFR ENROUTE LOW / HIGH ALTITUDE SYMBOLS
(U.S., PACIFIC AND ALASKA CHARTS)

AIRPORTS

Airport Data - Low/High Altitude

Civil	**Charts: High/Low**	Seaplane - Civil	**Charts: Low**

Civil And Military	**Charts: High/Low**	Heliport	**Charts: Low**

Military	**Charts: High/Low**	Emergency Use Only	Pacific Only

Facilities in BLUE or GREEN have an approved Instrument Approach Procedure and/or RADAR MINIMA published in either the FAA Terminal Procedures Publication or the DoD FLIPs. Those in BLUE have an Instrument Approach Procedure and/or RADAR MINIMA published at least in the High Altitude DoD FLIPs. Facilities in BROWN do not have a published Instrument Procedure or RADAR MINIMA.

All IAP Airports are shown on the Low Altitude Charts.

Non-IAP Airports shown on the U.S. Low Altitude Charts have a minimum hard surface runway of 3000'.

Airports shown on the U.S. High Altitude Charts have a minimum hard surface runway of 5000'.

Airports shown on the Alask High Altitude Charts have a minimum hard or soft surface runway of 4000'.

Associated city names for public airports are shown above or preceding the airport name and city name are the same only the airport name is shown. City names for military and private airports are not shown.

The airport identifier in parentheses follows the airport name or Pvt.

Pvt - Private Use

AIRPORT DATA DEPICTION

Low Altitude

1. Airport elevation given in feet above or below mean sea level

2. Pvt - Private use, not available to general public

3. A solid line box enclosed the airport name indicates FAR 93 Special Requirements - see Directory/Supplement

4. "NO SVFR" above the airport name indicates FAR 91 fixed-wing special VFR flight is prohibited.

5. C or D following the airport identifier indicates Class C or Class D Airspace

6. Associated city names for public airports are shown above or preceding the airport name. If airport name and city name are the same, only the airport name is shown. The airport identifier in parentheses follows the airport name. City names for military and private airports are not shown.

7. Airport Ident ICAO Location Indicator shown outside contiguous U.S.

8. AFIS Alaska only

High Altitude - Alaska

High Altitude - U.S.

69

Airports (Continued)

LIGHTING CAPABILITY

Lighting Available	L	Part-time or on request	★
Pilot Controlled Lighting	Ⓛ	No lighting available At private facilities- indicates no lighting information is available	-

RADIO AIDS TO NAVIGATION

NAVAIDS

	VOR	VOR/DME	TACAN	DME	NDB	NDB/DME	Reporting Function
	⬡	⬡̸	▽	☐	◉	◉	Non Compulsory Reporting or Off Airway
	⬢	⬢		■	●	●	Compulsory Reporting

Note: VHF/UHF is depicted in Black. LF/MF is depicted in Brown. RNAV is depicted in Blue

Compass Roses

VHF/UHF

LF/MF

Compass Roses are orientated to Magnetic North of the NAVAID which may not be adjusted to the charted isogonic values.

Compass Locator Beacon

LOW ALTITUDE

Chart Example : Enroute Low L-27 US

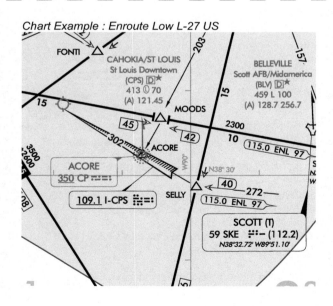

RADIO AIDS TO NAVIGATION (Continued)

ILS LOCALIZER

LOW ALTITUDE

ILS Localizer Course with additional navigation function

ILS Localizer Back Course with additional navigation function

VOR/DME RNAV WAYPOINT DATA

HIGH ALTITUDE - ALASKA

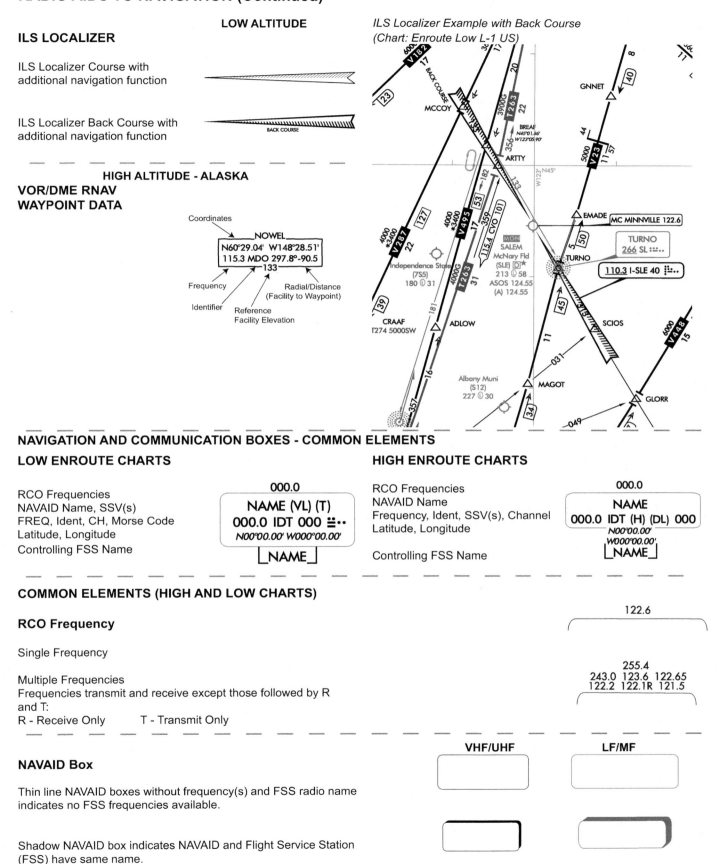

ILS Localizer Example with Back Course (Chart: Enroute Low L-1 US)

NAVIGATION AND COMMUNICATION BOXES - COMMON ELEMENTS

LOW ENROUTE CHARTS

RCO Frequencies
NAVAID Name, SSV(s)
FREQ, Ident, CH, Morse Code
Latitude, Longitude
Controlling FSS Name

```
        000.0
  NAME (VL) (T)
  000.0 IDT 000 ≝··
   N00°00.00' W000°00.00'
    ⌊NAME⌋
```

HIGH ENROUTE CHARTS

RCO Frequencies
NAVAID Name
Frequency, Ident, SSV(s), Channel
Latitude, Longitude

Controlling FSS Name

```
        000.0
        NAME
  000.0 IDT (H) (DL) 000
      N00°00.00'
      W000°00.00'
    ⌊NAME⌋
```

COMMON ELEMENTS (HIGH AND LOW CHARTS)

RCO Frequency

Single Frequency

Multiple Frequencies
Frequencies transmit and receive except those followed by R and T:
R - Receive Only   T - Transmit Only

```
        122.6
```

```
        255.4
   243.0  123.6  122.65
   122.2  122.1R  121.5
```

NAVAID Box

Thin line NAVAID boxes without frequency(s) and FSS radio name indicates no FSS frequencies available.

Shadow NAVAID box indicates NAVAID and Flight Service Station (FSS) have same name.

VHF/UHF

LF/MF

FAA Chart Users' Guide - IFR Enroute Symbology

RADIO AIDS TO NAVIGATION (Continued)

Navigation and Communication Boxes - Common Elements

NAVAID STANDARD SERVICE VOLUME (SSV) CLASSIFICATIONS

(VL), (T), etc. indicate SSV. See "NAVAID STANDARD SERVICE VOLUME (SSV) CLASSIFICATIONS" on page 62 or the Chart Supplement for SSV Altitude and Range Boundaries.

(VL) (T)

DISTANCE MEASURING EQUIPMENT

Facilities that operate in the "Y" mode for DME reception

(Y)

VOICE COMMUNICATIONS VIA NAVAID

Voice Transmitted

112.6

No Voice Transmitted

<u>111.0</u>

NAVAID SHUTDOWN STATUS

VHF/UHF   **LF/MF**

PART TIME OR ON-REQUEST

VHF/UHF   **LF/MF**
★   ★

AUTOMATED WEATHER BROADCAST SERVICES

ASOS/AWOS - Automated Surface Observing Station/Automated Weather Observing Station

VHF/UHF   LF/MF

Ⓐ   Ⓐ

LATITUDE AND LONGITUDE

Latitude and Longitude coordinates are provided for those NAVAIDs that make up part of a route/airway or a holding pattern. All TACAN facilities will include geographic coordinates.

LOW ENROUTE   **HIGH ENROUTE**

N00°00.00' W000°00.00'   *N00°00.00'*
                              W000°00.00'

Navigation and Communication Boxes - Examples

LOW ENROUTE CHARTS

VOR

R - Receive only 122.1R

Controlling FSS Name - ANDERSON

```
      122.1R
   ALLENDALE
 116.7 ALD ▯▦·•
 N33°00.75' W81°17.53'
 ⌊ANDERSON⌋
```

(T) - Service Volume

```
   POLK (T)
 108.4 FXU ▦▯·
```

Receive & Transmit on 122.35
(T) - Service Volume
Latitude and Longitude
Controlling FSS Name - MACON

```
      122.35
 TIFT MYERS (T)
 112.5 IFM ▯▦·•
 N31°25.72' W83°29.33'
 ⌊MACON⌋
```

HIGH ENROUTE CHARTS

VOR

```
   CECIL
 117.9 VQQ
 N30°12.78'
 W81°53.45'
```

RADIO AIDS TO NAVIGATION (Continued)

Navigation And Communication Boxes - Examples (Continued)

LOW ENROUTE CHARTS | HIGH ENROUTE CHARTS

VOR/DME

No Voice Communications
(Y) Mode DME

> SAWMILL
> 113.75 SWB 84(Y)

R - Receive only 122.1R
Controlling FSS Name - BUFFALO

> 122.1R
> ROCKDALE
> 112.6 RKA 73
> N42°27.98' W75°14.36'
> BUFFALO

Shadow NAVAID Box
FSS Associated with NAVAID

> 119.1
> MIRABEL
> 116.7 YMX 114
> N45°53.30' W74°22.54'

VOR/DME

Off Route (Greyed NAVAID Box
and NAVAID)

> ITHACA
> 111.8 ITH (L) (DL) 55

Service Volume - L
DME in Y Mode

> ELMIRA
> 109.65 ULW (L) 33(Y)
> N42°05.65'
> W77°01.49'

Shadow NAVAID Box
FSS Associated with NAVAID

> 119.1
> MIRABEL
> 116.7 YMX 114
> N45°53.30'
> W74°22.54'

TACAN

TACAN Channels are without
voice but not underlined

> SANTA ROSA
> 63 NGS · (133.6)
> N30°36.91' W86°56.24'

Part Time NAVAID

> PENSACOLA
> ★119 NPA · (117.2)
> N30°21.48' W87°18.99'

TACAN

Off Route

> TYNDALL
> 64 PAM (133.7)
> N30°04.44'
> W85°34.34'

Off Route - Part Time NAVAID
(Greyed NAVAID Box and NAVAID)
Service Volume - L

> PENSACOLA
> 119 NPA (L) (117.2)
> N30°21.48'
> W87°18.99'

VORTAC

> 255.4 243.0 122.55 121.5
> ALEXANDRIA
> 116.1 AEX 108
> N31°15.40' W92°30.06'
> DE RIDDER

Shutdown status

> BRUNSWICK
> NHZ ·
> N43°52.41' W69°55.31'

VORTAC

> 122.55
> ALEXANDRIA
> 116.1 AEX 108
> N31°15.40'
> W92°30.06'
> DE RIDDER

Off Route (Greyed NAVAID Box
and NAVAID)
Service Volume - L

> HANDLE
> 114.3 HLL (L) (DL) 90

DME

DME Channel, Ident, Morse Code,
VHF Frequency

> MOULTRIE
> 25 MGR · (108.8)
> N31°04.94' W83°48.25'

DME

DME Channel, Ident,
VHF Frequency

> DUNKIRK
> 109 DKK (116.2)

NDB

A - ASOS/AWOS Available

> SILVER BAY Ⓐ
> 350 BFW

Shutdown status

> SHEMYA
> SYA · –
> N52°43.32' E174°03.62'

NDB

> FORT DAVIS
> 529 FDV
> N64°29.68'
> W165°18.91'

NDB/DME

No Voice Communications
(Y) Mode DME

> 122.3
> CAPE LISBURNE
> 385 LUR 20(Y) (108.35)
> N68°52.28' W166°04.56'
> KOTZEBUE

Shadow NAVAID Box
FSS Associated with NAVAID

> 123.6
> ILIAMNA
> 411 ILI 91 (114.4)
> N59°44.88' W154°54.58'

NDB/DME

No Voice Communications
(Y) Mode DME

> CAPE NEWENHAM
> 385 EHM 18(Y) (108.15)
> N58°39.36'
> W162°04.42'

Shadow NAVAID Box
FSS Associated with NAVAID

> ILIAMNA
> 411 ILI 91 (114.4)

Notes:

Notes: *Morse Code is not shown on High NAVAID Boxes.*

FAA Chart Users' Guide - IFR Enroute Symbology

RADIO AIDS TO NAVIGATION (Continued)

Stand Alone Flight Services and Communication Outlets

LOW CHARTS   **HIGH CHARTS**

Flight Service Station (FSS)

Shadow NAVAID boxes indicate Flight Service Station (FSS) locations. Frequencies 122.2 and 255.4 (Conterminous U.S.); 121.5, 122.2, 243.0 and 255.4 (Alaska); and 121.5, 126.7, and 243.0 (Canada) are available at many FSSs and are not shown. All other frequencies are shown above the box.

Certain FSSs provide Local Airport Advisory (LAA) on 123.6.

Frequencies transmit and receive except those followed by R and T:
R - Receive Only
T - Transmit Only

Stand Alone FSS

> 122.55
> **DAYTON DAY**

Stand Alone FSS

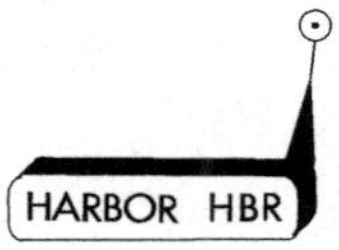

> **HARBOR HBR**

Stand Alone FSS Associated with an Airport

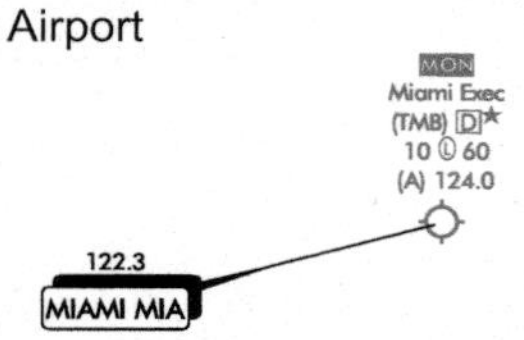

> MON
> Miami Exec
> (TMB) [D] ★
> 10 ⓛ 60
> (A) 124.0
>
> 122.3
> **MIAMI MIA**

Stand Alone FSS Associated with an Airport

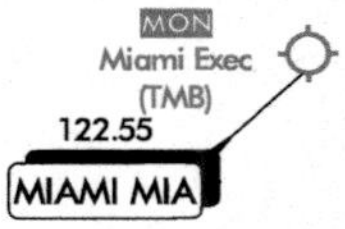

> MON
> Miami Exec
> (TMB)
> 122.55
> **MIAMI MIA**

Part-time FSS

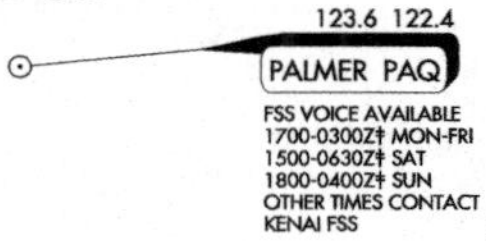

> 123.6 122.4
> **PALMER PAQ**
> FSS VOICE AVAILABLE
> 1700-0300Z‡ MON-FRI
> 1500-0630Z‡ SAT
> 1800-0400Z‡ SUN
> OTHER TIMES CONTACT
> KENAI FSS

Stand Alone FSS within Canadian Airspace

> 122.2
> **VICTORIA HARBOUR**
> FSS AVAILABLE 1345-0530Z‡

Stand Alone FSS within Canadian Airspace

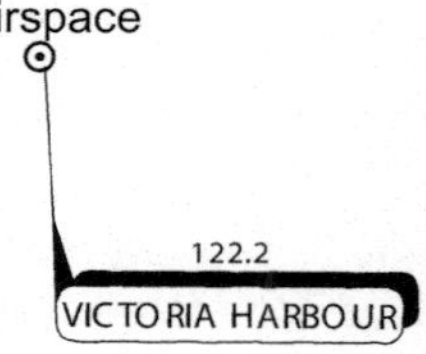

> 122.2
> **VICTORIA HARBOUR**

Remote Communications Outlet (RCO)

Thin line NAVAID boxes without frequencies and controlling FSS name indicate no FSS frequencies available. Frequencies positioned above the thin line boxes are remoted to the NAVAID sites. Other frequencies at the controlling FSS named are available, however altitude and terrain may determine their reception.

In Canada, a "D" after the frequency indicates a dial-up remote communications outlet.

Stand Alone RCO

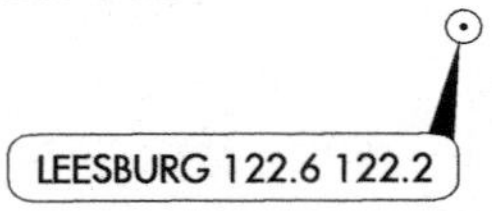

> **LEESBURG 122.6 122.2**

Stand Alone RCO

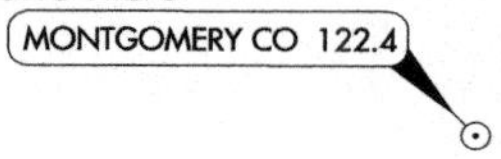

> **MONTGOMERY CO 122.4**

RCO Associated/Co-located with an Airport

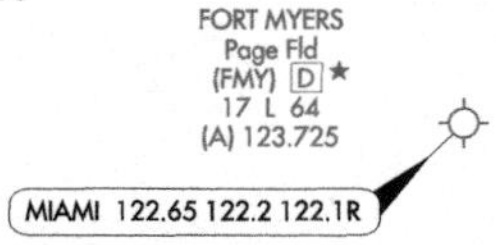

> FORT MYERS
> Page Fld
> (FMY) [D] ★
> 17 L 64
> (A) 123.725
>
> **MIAMI 122.65 122.2 122.1R**

RCO Associated/Co-located with an Airport

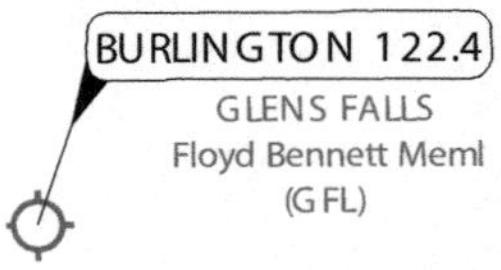

> **BURLINGTON 122.4**
> GLENS FALLS
> Floyd Bennett Meml
> (GFL)

Stand Alone AWOS & ASOS

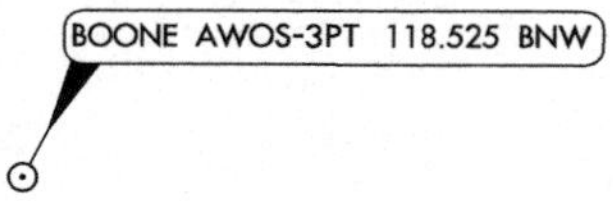

> **BOONE AWOS-3PT 118.525 BNW**

> **STAMPEDE PASS ASOS 135.275 SMP**

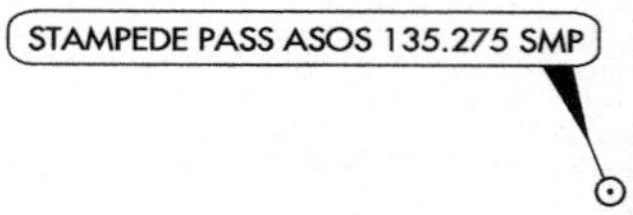

FAA Chart Users' Guide - IFR Enroute Symbology

AIRSPACE INFORMATION

Airway/Route Types
Low and High Enroute Airway Data:

VHF/UHF Data is depicted in Black.
LF/MF Data is depicted in Brown.
RNAV Route data is depicted in Blue

Low Enroute Charts

Victor Airways — V 0 —

LF/MF Airway A0

Uncontrolled LF/MF Airway - A0 - -

RNAV T Route — T000 —

GNSS Required

RNAV TK Helicopter Route — TK000 —

GNSS Required

Preferred Single Direction Victor Route V 0 ▶

Unusable Route Segment /\/\/\/\

Direction of Flight Indicator Canadian Routes Only ◄ EVEN

Military Training Routes (MTR)

MTRs 5NM or less both sides of centerline
IR-000 →
VR-000 →

MTRs greater than 5NM either or both sides of centerline
IR-000 →
VR-000 →

Arrow indicates direction of route

See MTR tabulation for altitude range information

All IR and VR MTRs are shown except those VRs at or bleow 1500' AGL

CAUTION: Inset charts do not depict MTRs

High Enroute Charts

Jet Routes — J000 —

Atlantic Routes — AR0 — AR0 —

Bahama Routes — BROL — BROL —

RNAV Q Routes — Q00 —

Alaska Q Routes require GNSS and radar surveillance. Within the CONUS, GNSS or DME/DME/IRU RNAV required, unless otherwise indicated. DME/DME/IRU aircraft require radar surveillance.

Preferred Single Direction Jet Routes J0 ▶

Preferred Single Direction RNAV Q Routes Q0 ▶

Single Direction ATS Route R000 ▶

Unusable Route Segment /\/\/\/\

Low and High Enroute Charts

ATS Route A0   A0

Oceanic Route — A00 — A00 —

Substitute Route

All relative and supporting data shown in brown.

See NOTAMs or appropriate publication for specific information.

FAA Chart Users' Guide - IFR Enroute Symbology

Airspace Information (Continued)

FIXES		REPORTING FUNCTION	WAYPOINTS RNAV
VHF/UHF	LF/MF		
▲	▲	**Compulsory Position Reporting**	◆
△	△	**Non-Compulsory Position Reporting**	◇
N25°46.47′ **W76°16.28′**	N29°36.00′ W88°01.00′	**Fix or Waypoint Coordinates** *Fix Coordinates are shown for compulsory, offshore and holding fixes.* *Waypoints Coordinates are shown when waypoint is not part of a RNAV route and when located on or beyond the boundary of the U.S. Continental Control (12 mile limit).*	N44°25.36′ W64°11.00′
		Off-set arrows indicate facility forming a fix *- Arrow points away from the VHF/UHF NAVAID* *- Arrow points towards the LF/MF NAVAID*	N/A
		Distance Measuring Equipment (DME) Fix *Denotes DME fix (distance same as airway / route mileage)*	N/A
VHF/UHF [15]→		**Distance Measuring Equipment (DME) Fix** *Denotes DME fix (encircled mileage shown when not otherwise obvious)*	**RNAV** N/A
5 → 10 [15] →		**Example:** *First segment, 5NM; second segment 10NM; total milage provided in encircled DME arrow.*	N/A
VHF/UHF [229]	**LF/MF** [149]	**Total Mileages between Compulsory Reporting Points or NAVAIDs** *Note: All mileages are in Nautical Miles*	**RNAV** N/A
54	125	**MILEAGE BETWEEN OTHER FIXES, NAVAIDs AND/OR MILEAGE BREAKDOWN**	125
X (AFWOX)	X (MSABI)	**Mileage Breakdown or Computer Navigation Fix (CNF)** *Five letter identifier in parentheses indicates CNF with no ATC function*	N/A
000.0 IDT 000 000.0 IDT 000	000 ID 000 ID	**FACILITY LOCATOR BOATS** *Crosshatch indicates Shutdown status of NAVAID*	N/A
← 000 —	N/A	**RADIAL OUTBOUND FROM A VHF/UHF NAVAID** *All Radials are magnetic.*	N/A
N/A	— 000 →	**BEARING INBOUND TO AN LF/MF NAVAID** *All Bearings are magnetic.*	N/A
N/A	N/A	**MAGNETIC REFERENCE BEARING**, outbound from a NAVAID or Fix *Note: Not shown on joint Victor/RNAV or Jet/RNAV Routes.*	000 →

FAA Chart Users' Guide - IFR Enroute Symbology

Airspace Information (Continued)

VHF/UHF	LF/MF		RNAV

MINIMUM ENROUTE ALTITUDE (MEA)
All Altitudes Are MSL Unless Otherwise Noted.

VHF/UHF LOW CHARTS: 0000
LF/MF LOW CHARTS: 0000
RNAV LOW CHARTS: 0000G

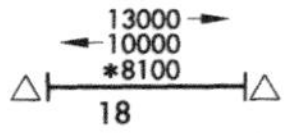

13000 →
← 10000
△ ⊢ *8100 ⊣ △
18

Directional MEAs

VHF/UHF HIGH CHARTS: MEA-29000
LF/MF HIGH CHARTS: MEA-FL240

MEAs are shown on IFR High Altitude Charts when MEA is other than 18,000'.

RNAV HIGH CHARTS:

MEA for GNSS RNAV aircraft
MEA-24000G

MEA for DME/DME/IRU RNAV aircraft
MEA-24000D

MINIMUM ENROUTE ALTITUDE (MEA) GAP

MEA is established when there is a gap in navigation signal coverage.

RNAV: N/A

LOW CHARTS
15000
13300G
*13300
V 465   MEA GAP   51
35 114   63

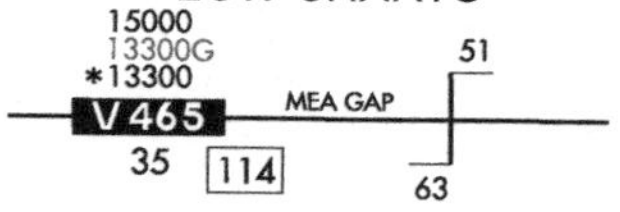

HIGH CHARTS
MEA GAP   TWISP △   MEA-24000   J505
65   108   91   279

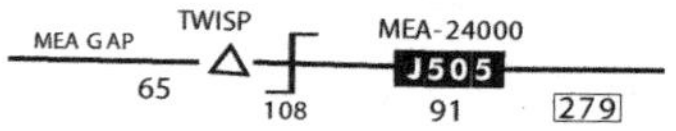

Maximum Authorized Altitude (MAA)
All Altitudes Are MSL Unless Otherwise Noted.

MAAs are shown on IFR High Altitude Charts when MAA is other than 45,000'.

LOW / HIGH CHARTS:
VHF/UHF: MAA-00000
LF/MF: MAA-00000
RNAV: MAA-00000

Minimum Obstruction Clearance Altitude (MOCA)

All Altitudes Are MSL Unless Otherwise Noted.

LOW CHARTS:
VHF/UHF: *0000
LF/MF: *0000
RNAV: *0000

Minimum Turning Altitude (MTA) and Minimum Crossing Altitude (MCA)

See Low Enroute Chart Example below for examples of both MTAs and MCAs.

LOW CHARTS — flag symbol with X

MINIMUM RECEPTION ALTITUDE (MRA)

Flag symbol with R

RNAV: N/A

ALTITUDE CHANGE
MEA, MOCA and/or MAA change at other than NAVAIDs

⊣ ⊢

CHANGEOVER POINT

LOW / HIGH CHARTS:
00 / 00

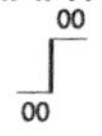

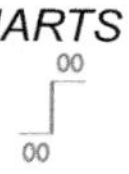

RNAV: N/A

Changeover Point giving mileage to NAVAIDs (Not shown at midpoint locations.)

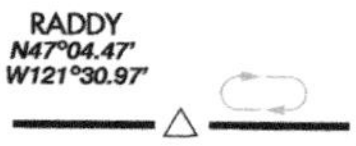

HOLDING PATTERNS
RNAV Holding Pattern Magnetic Reference Bearing is determined by the isogonic value at the waypoint or fix.

Holding Pattern with maximum restriction airspeed 210K applies to altitudes 6000' to and including 14000'. 175K applied to all altitudes. Airspeed depicted is Indicated Airspeed (IAS)

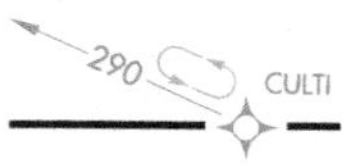

RADDY
N47°04.47'
W121°30.97'

LARGE
N39°17.12'
W89°18.07'

210K

290 CULTI

Enroute Chart Examples
Low Enroute Chart

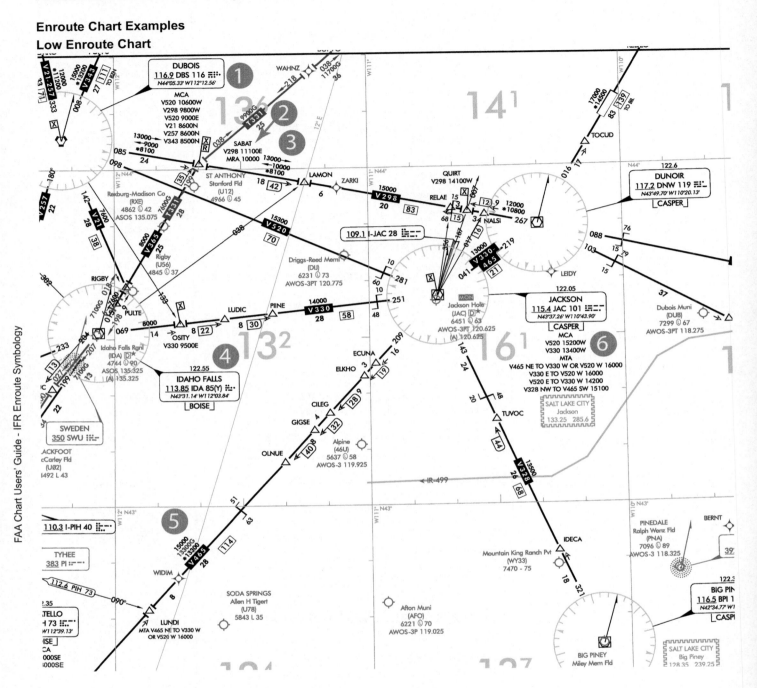

FAA Chart Users' Guide - IFR Enroute Symbology

AIRSPACE INFORMATION (Continued)

Enroute Chart Examples
Low Enroute Chart (Continued)

Reference Number	Description

①

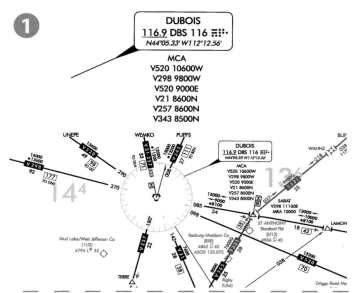

Multiple MCAs at a NAVAID

V21 and V257 - MCA at DBS of 8600' traveling North
V298 - MCA at DBS of 9800' traveling West
V343 - MCA at DBS of 8500' traveling North
V520 - MCA at DBS of 9000' traveling East
V520 - MCA at DBS of 10600' traveling West

---

②

MCA and MRA at a Fix

MCA at SABAT on V298 of 11,100 traveling East.
MRA at SABAT of 10000.

---

③

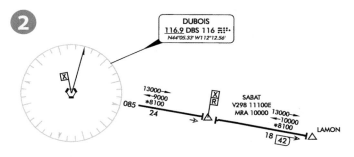

Example of MOCA and directional MEAs along a Victor Route

Traveling East from DBS, MEA 13,000' the first two segments, 15,000 along third segment.

Traveling West from QUIRT, MEA of 15,000' the first segment, MEA of 10,000 the second segment and MEA of 9,000 the third segment.

MOCA for DBS to SABAT and SABAT to LAMON segments of 8100

---

④

MCA Example

MCA at OSITY on V330. MCA of 9500' traveling East on V330 from Idaho Falls (IDA) VOR-DME.

AIRSPACE INFORMATION (Continued)

Enroute Chart Examples

Low Enroute Chart (Continued)

Reference Number	Description

MEA VHF and RNAV Example

MEA for aircraft utilizing VHF NAVAID of 15000'
MEA for aircraft utilizing RNAV of 13300'

MOCA of 13300'

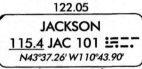

MCA and MTA Example at a NAVAID

MCA for aircraft traveling West along V520 to cross JAC at 15200'
MCA for aircraft traveling West along V330 to cross JAC at 13400'

MTA for aircraft crossing over and turning at JAC:

Aircraft traveling NE on V465 and turning to V330 on a W heading or turning to V520 on a W heading must turn at altitude of 16000' or higher

Aircraft traveling E on V520 and turning to V330 on a W heading must turn at altitude of 14200'

Aircraft traveling E on V330 and turning to V520 on a W heading must turn at altitude of 16000' or higher

Aircraft traveling NW on V328 and turning to V465 on a SW heading must turn at altitude of 15100' or higher.

Airspace Information (Continued)

Enroute Chart Examples
High Enroute Chart

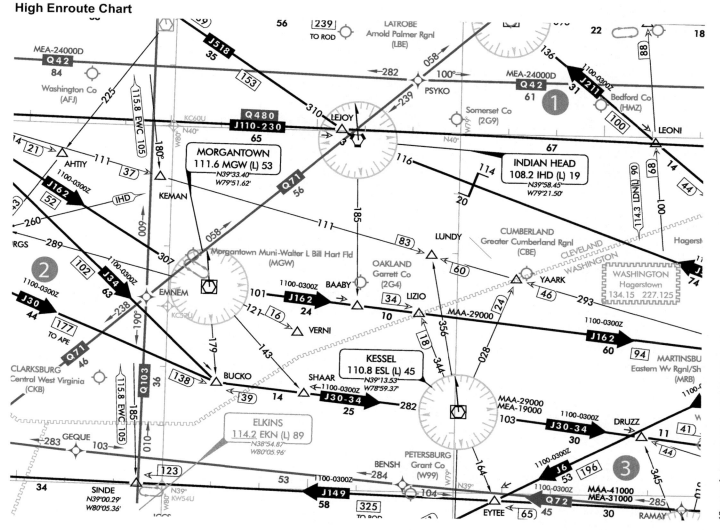

FAA Chart Users' Guide - IFR Enroute Symbology

Reference Number

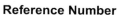

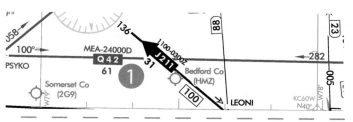

Description

High RNAV Route with MEA for DME/DME/IRU RNAV Aircraft

MEA of 24,000'

Directional Jet Route with Time Restrictions

Jet Route 34 available between 1100 - 0300Z

AIRSPACE INFORMATION (Continued)

Enroute Chart Examples
High Enroute Chart (Continued)

Reference Number	Description
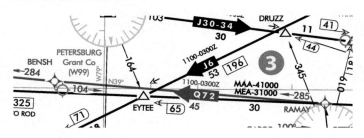	**Directional Jet Route with Time Restrictions, MAA and MEA** Jet Route 149 available between 1100 - 0300Z MAA - 41,000' MEA - 31,000'

AIRSPACE BOUNDARIES

Air Defense Identification Zone (ADIZ)

LOW / HIGH CHARTS

CONTIGUOUS U.S. ADIZ

ALASKA ADIZ

CANADA ADIZ

Adjoining ADIZ

Air Traffic Service Identification Data

LOW / HIGH CHARTS

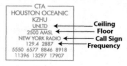

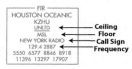

Flight Information Regions (FIR)

LOW / HIGH CHARTS

TORONTO FIR CZYZ

MONTREAL FIR CZUL

TORONTO FIR CZYZ

Upper Information Regions (UIR)

Upper Control Areas (UTA)

Air Route Traffic Control Center (ARTCC)

LOW / HIGH CHARTS

ARTCC Remoted Sites with discrete VHF and UHF frequencies

NEW YORK
WASHINGTON

NEW YORK ← ARTCC Name
Barnegat ← Site Name
132.15 ← Frequency

Air Route Traffic Control Center (ARTCC) with Controller Pilot Data Link Communications (CPDLC)

ATLANTA
JACKSONVILLE
CPDLC (LOGON KUSA)

CPDLC (LOGON KUSA)
ATLANTA
JACKSONVILLE
CPDLC (LOGON KUSA)

Altimeter Setting Change

QNH
ALTIMETER
QNE 29.92

Control Areas (CTA)

LOW / HIGH CHARTS

NEW YORK OCEANIC CTA/FIR KZWY

MIAMI OCEANIC CTA/FIR KZMA

Adjoining CTA

Additional Control Areas

LOW ALTITUDE

CONTROL 1141L

HIGH ALTITUDE

CONTROL 1419 H

AIRSPACE INFORMATION (Continued)

Airspace - U.S.

Class A

High Chart Only

Controlled Airspace

Open Area (White)

That airspace from 18,000' MSL to and including FL 600, including the airspace overflying the waters within 12 NM of the coast of the contiguous United States and Alaska and designated offshore areas, excluding Santa Barbara Island, Farallon Island, the airspace south of latitude 25° 04'00" N, the Alaska peninsula west of longitude 160°00'00" W, and the airspace less than 1,500' AGL.

That airspace from 18,000' MSL to and including FL 450, including Santa Barbara Island, Farallon Island, the Alaska peninsula west of longitude 160°00'00" W, and designated offshore areas.

Class B

Low Chart Only

Controlled Airspace

Screened Blue with a Solid Blue Outline

Example:

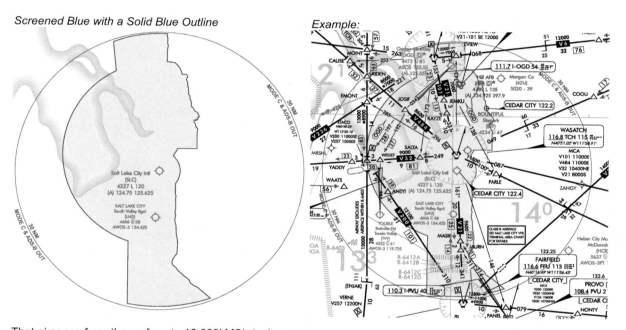

That airspace from the surface to 10,000' MSL (unless otherwise designated) surrounding the nation's busiest airports. Each Class B airspace area is individually tailored and consists of a surface area and two or more layers.

Mode C Area

Low Chart Only

Controlled Airspace

A Solid Blue Outline

That airspace within 30 NM of the primary airports of Class B airspace and within 10 NM of designated airports. Mode-C transponder and ADS-B Out equipment is required. (See FAR 91.215)

Example:

See Chart example above.

FAA Chart Users' Guide - IFR Enroute Symbology

AIRSPACE INFORMATION (Continued)

Airspace - U.S. (Continued)

CLASS C

Low Chart Only

Controlled Air-space

Screened Blue with a Solid Blue Dashed Outline

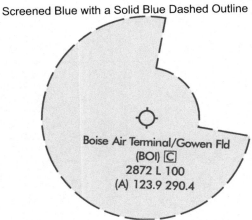

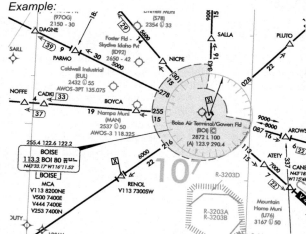

Example:

That airspace from the surface to 4,000' (unless otherwise designated) above the elevation of selected airports (charted in MSL). The normal radius of the outer limits of Class C airspace is 10NM. Class C airspace is also indicated by the letter C in a box following the airport name.

CLASS D

Low Chart Only

Controlled Air-space

Open Area (White)

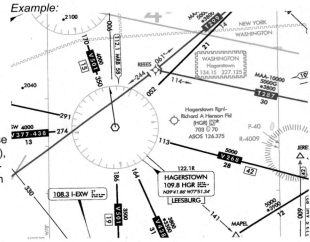

Example:

That airspace from the surface to 2,500' unless otherwise designated) above the airport elevation (charted in MSL), surrounding those airports that have an operational control tower. Class D airspace is indicated by the letter D in a box following the airport name.

CLASS E

Low Chart Only

Controlled Air-space

Open Area (White)

That controlled airspace below 14,500' MSL which is not Class B, C or D.

Federal Airways from 1,200' AGL to but not including 18,000' MSL (unless otherwise specified).

Other designated control areas below 14,500' MSL.

Not Charted

That airspace from 14,500' MSL to but not including 18,000' MSL, including the airspace overflying the waters within 12 NM of the coast of the contiguous United States and Alaska and designated offshore areas, excluding the Alaska peninsula west of longitude 160°00'00" W, and the airspace less than 1,500' AGL.

Airspace Information (Continued)

AIRSPACE - U.S.

CLASS G

High and Low Chart

Uncontrolled Airspace

Screened Brown Area

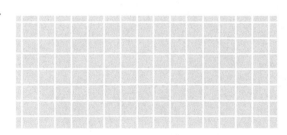

Low Altitude

That portion of the airspace below 14,500' MSL that has not been designated as Class B, C, D or E Airspace.

High Altitude

That portion of the airspace from 18,000' MSL and above that has not been designated as Class A airspace.

Example:

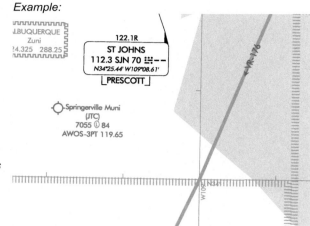

AIRSPACE - CANADIAN

CLASS B

Low Charts Only

Controlled Airspace

Screened Brown Checkered Area

Controlled airspace above 12,500' MSL

Example:

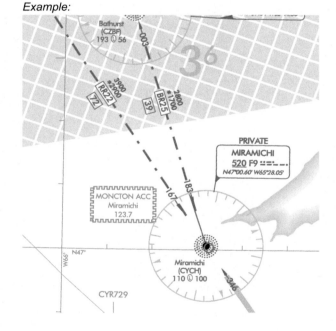

FAA Chart Users' Guide - IFR Enroute Symbology

AIRSPACE INFORMATION (Continued)

Special Use Airspace - U.S.

Low and High Charts

P - Prohibited Area

Example: P-56 -
Washington DC, Area A-1 Chart

Example: P-40 and R-4009 -
Washington DC, Area A-1 Chart

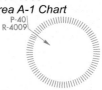

R - Restricted Area

Example: R3601A -

W - Warning Area

Example: W-50

See Airspace Tabulation on each chart for complete documentation information on:

Area Identification
Effective Altitude
Operating Times
Controlling Agency Voice Call

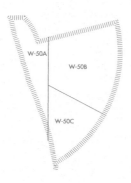

Low Charts Only

A - Alert Area

* Alert Areas do not extend into Class A, B, C and D airspace, or Class E airport surface areas.

MOA - Military Operations Area

See Airspace Tabulation on each chart for complete documentation information on:
Area Identification
Effective Altitude
Operating Times
Controlling Agency Voice Call

AIRSPACE INFORMATION (Continued)

Off Route Obstruction Clearance Altitude (OROCA)

Low Charts Only OROCA is computed similarly to the Maximum Elevation Figure (MEF) found on Visual charts except that it provides an additional vertical buffer of 1,000 feet in designated non-mountainous areas and a 2,000 foot vertical buffer in designated mountainous areas within the United States.

Example: 12,500 feet

$$12^5$$

Example: Low L-13 Chart

Special Flight Rules Area (SFRA)

Low and High Charts SFRA Symbology

Example: Low Chart (Washington Area Chart)

Example: High Chart (H-12)

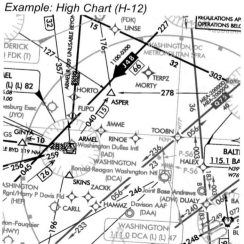

AIRSPACE INFORMATION (Continued)

Special Use Airspace - Canada & Caribbean

Low and High Charts

Canada Only

CYA - Advisory Area

CYD - Danger Area

CYR - Restricted Area

Caribbean Only
D - Danger Area

In the Caribbean, the first two letters represent the country code, i.e. (MY) Bahamas, (MU) Cuba

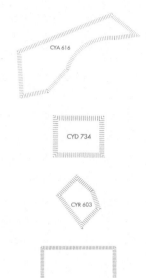

NAVIGATIONAL AND PROCEDURAL INFORMATION

Cruising Altitudes - Low Charts - U.S. Only

IFR outside controlled airspace.

IFR within controlled airspace as assigned by ATC.

ALL courses are magnetic.

VFR above 3000' AGL unless otherwise authorized by ATC.

Cruising Altitudes - High Charts - U.S. Only

IFR within controlled airspace as assigned by ATC

All courses are magnetic.

18,000' MSL to FL280

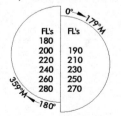

VFR or VFR On Top add 500'

No VFR flights within Class A Airspace above 3000' AGL unless otherwise authorized

RVSM Levels FL290 to FL410

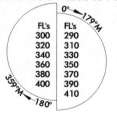

No VFR or VFR On Top authorized above FL285 in RVSM airspace.

FL430 and above

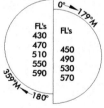

Navigational and Procedural Information (Continued)

FAA Chart Users' Guide - IFR Enroute Symbology

ISOGONIC LINE AND VALUE

LOW/HIGH CHARTS

10°W

ENLARGEMENT AREA

SEE WASHINGTON AREA CHART A-1 FOR DETAIL

MORSE CODE

A	.—	F	..—.	K	—.—	P	.——.	U	..—
B	—...	G	——.	L	.—..	Q	——.—	V	...—
C	—.—.	H	....	M	——	R	.—.	W	.——
D	—..	I	..	N	—.	S	...	X	—..—
E	.	J	.———	O	———	T	—	Y	—.——
								Z	——..

1	.————
2	..———
3	...——
4	....—
5	.....
6	—....
7	——...
8	———..
9	————.
0	—————

TIME ZONE

All time is Coordinated Universal Time (UTC)

Mountain Std
+7 = UTC

Central Std
+6 = UTC

During periods of Day-lights Savings Time (DT), effective hours will be one hour earlier than shown. All states observe DT except Arizona and Hawaii

MATCH MARK

LOW/HIGH CHARTS

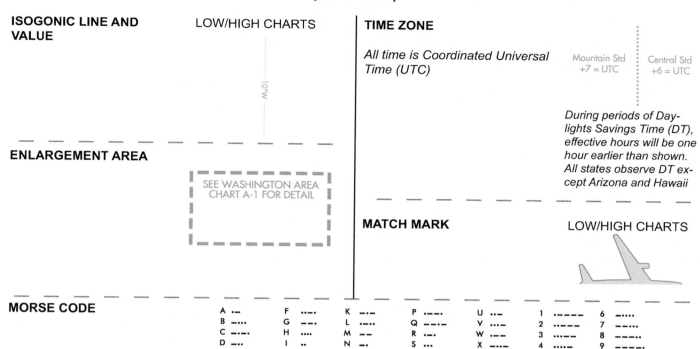

CULTURE

Boundaries

International

LOW/HIGH ALTITUDE

(Not shown when coincident with ARTCC or FIR)

U.S./Russia Maritime Line

LOW/HIGH ALTITUDE

RUSSIA
UNITED STATES

Date Line

LOW/HIGH ALTITUDE

INTERNATIONAL DATELINE

SUNDAY
MONDAY

HYDROGRAPHY

SHORELINES

TOPOGRAPHY

TERRAIN
Area Charts

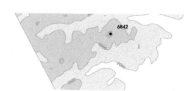

6842

U.S. TERMINAL PROCEDURES PUBLICATION

The U.S. Terminal Procedures Publication (TPPs) includes the Instrument Approach Procedures (IAPs), Departure Procedures (DPs) charts, Standard Terminal Arrival (STAR) charts, Charted Visual Flight Procedure (CVFP) charts, and Airport Diagrams. Also included are Takeoff Minimums, (Obstacle) Departure Procedures, Diverse Vector Area (RADAR Vectors), RADAR and Alternate Minimum textual procedures.

EXPLANATION OF TPP TERMS AND SYMBOLS

The information and examples in this section are based primarily on the IFR (Instrument Flight Rules) Terminal Procedures Publication (TPP). The publication legends list aeronautical symbols with a brief description of what each symbol depicts. This section will provide more detailed information of some of the symbols and how they are used on TPP charts.

FAA Terminal charts are prepared in accordance with specifications of the Interagency Air Committee (IAC) and their supporting technical groups for the purpose of standardization, which are approved by representatives of the Federal Aviation Administration (FAA), and the Department of Defense (DoD).

The Terminal Procedure Publication is made up of the following charts:

- Instrument Approach Procedure (IAP) Charts
- Airport Diagrams
- Departure Procedures (DP)
- Standard Terminal Arrival (STAR) Charts
- Charted Visual Flight Procedure (CVFP) Charts

INSTRUMENT APPROACH PROCEDURE CHART

The IAPs (charts) are divided into various sections:

Margin Identification Information

Briefing Strip Information

Planview

Missed Approach Information

Profile View

Landing Minimums

Airport Sketch

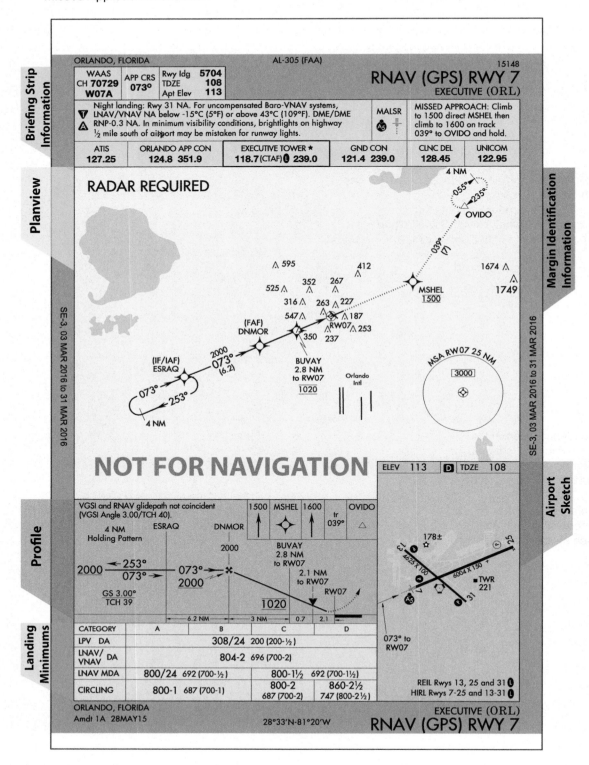

Margin Identification Information

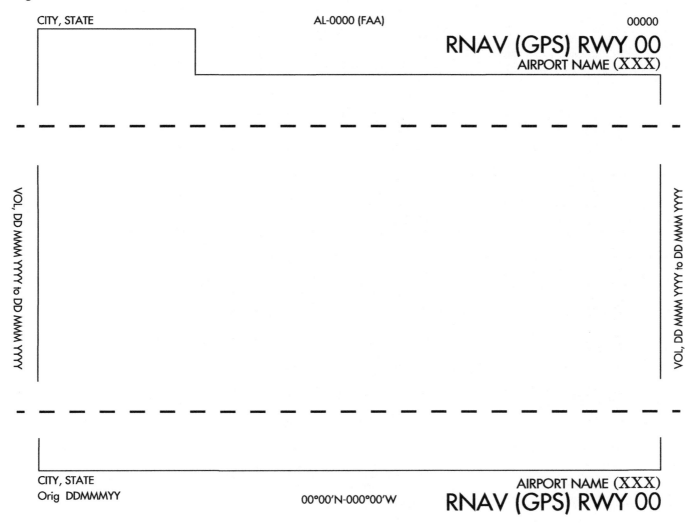

CITY, STATE   AL-0000 (FAA)   00000

RNAV (GPS) RWY 00
AIRPORT NAME (XXX)

VOL, DD MMM YYYY to DD MMM YYYY

VOL, DD MMM YYYY to DD MMM YYYY

CITY, STATE
Orig DDMMMYY   00°00'N-000°00'W

AIRPORT NAME (XXX)
RNAV (GPS) RWY 00

FAA Chart Users' Guide - Terminal Procedures Publication (TPP) - Terms

The margin identification at the top, bottom, and sides of the chart provides information about the airport location, procedure identification, and chart currency. The charts are organized by city first, then airport name and state, with the exception of military charts, which are organized by airport name. Going from the top of the chart, reading from left to right, and going down the chart, Margin Identification Information is organized in the following way.

The hash marks along the top and bottom borders of military Instrument Approach Charts indicate that the procedure was designed using High Altitude criteria contained in FAA Order 8260.3. These procedures are designed to support high performance military aircraft operations and are not intended for civilian use.

Top Margin Information:

The city and state with which the airport is associated is located on both the top and bottom margins.

At the center of the top margin is the FAA numbering system. This Approach and Landing (AL) number is followed by the organization responsible for the procedure in parentheses, e.g., AL-18 (FAA), AL-227 (USAF).

WASHINGTON, DC   AL-5326 (FAA)   15344

WAAS	APP CRS	Rwy Idg	3715
CH **56239**	**326°**	TDZE	**182**
W34B		Apt Elev	**192**

RNAV (GPS) RWY 34L
MANASSAS RGNL/HARRY P DAVIS FLD (HEF)

The procedure title is located on both the top and bottom margins. It is derived from the type of navigational facility that is providing the final approach course guidance. The title is abbreviated, e.g. ILS, RNAV, NDB, etc. For airports with parallel runways and simultaneous approach procedures, "L", "R" or "C" follows the runway number to distinguish between left, right, and center runways.

The airport name is shown on both the top and bottom margins below the procedure title. The airport identifier is shown in parentheses following the airport name. Airports outside the contiguous United States will be shown with the FAA designated identifier followed by the ICAO location identifier.

The Date of Latest Revision is shown on the top margin above the procedure title. The Date of Latest Revision identifies the Julian date the chart was last revised for any reason. The first two digits indicate the year, the last three digits indicate the day of the year (001 to 365/6).

WASHINGTON, DC   AL-5326 (FAA)   15344

WAAS	APP CRS	Rwy Idg	3715
CH **56239**	**326°**	TDZE	**182**
W34B		Apt Elev	**192**

RNAV (GPS) RWY 34L
MANASSAS RGNL/HARRY P DAVIS FLD (HEF)

15344
Year|Day of Year

Side Margin Information:

The side margins show the volume identification, i.e. SW-3, followed by the current issue date and the next issue date, e.g. SW-3, 21 JUL 2016 to 15 SEP 2016.

Bottom Margin Information:

The FAA Procedure Amendment Number, located on the left bottom margin below the City, State, represents the most current amendment of a given procedure. The Procedure Amendment Effective Date represents the AIRAC cycle date on which the procedure amendment was incorporated into the chart. Updates to the amendment number and effective date represent procedural/criteria revisions to the charted procedure, e.g., course, fix, altitude, minima, etc.

Example: Original Procedure Date

WASHINGTON, DC   MANASSAS RGNL/HARRY P DAVIS FLD (HEF)
Orig 10DEC15   38°43'N-77°31'W   **RNAV (GPS) RWY 34L**

Example: Amendment Procedure Date

WASHINGTON D.C.   MANASSAS RGNL/HARRY P DAVIS FLD (HEF)
Amdt 1B 28MAY15   38°43'N-77°31'W   **RNAV (GPS) RWY 16R**

The coordinates for the airport reference point are located at the center of the bottom margin.

BRIEFING STRIP INFORMATION

At the top of every TPP is the Briefing Strip which consists of three stacked strips of information immediately above the planview. Information varies depending upon the type of procedure.

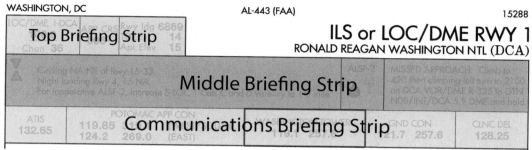

Top Briefing Strip

The top briefing strip contains procedural information in three separate boxes, in the following sequence from left to right:

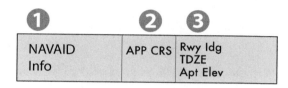

- **Box 1: Primary Procedure Navigation Information:** The primary navigation type (VOR, LOC, NDB, RNAV, etc.) with its identifier and frequency/channel. If applicable, WAAS, the WAAS Channel Number, and the WAAS Reference Path indicator are shown stacked top to bottom. If the primary navigation type is GBAS, then the following information is shown, stacked top to bottom: GBAS, CH NNNN, RPI XXXX. If there is not a primary Navigation Box required, the first box is removed.

- **Box 2: Final Approach Course Information.** The inbound Approach Course (APP CRS) is shown.

- **Box 3: Runway Landing Information:** Stacked top to bottom, the runway landing distance (Rwy Ldg), the Touchdown Zone Elevation (TDZE), and the Airport Elevation (Apt Elev) are shown. Rwy Ldg may not reflect full runway length due to displaced thresholds and shorter declared distances.

Top Briefing Strip Examples:

Ground based NAVAID:

DENVER, COLORADO				16147
LOC/DME I-DZG **111.55** Chan **52**(Y)	APP CRS **082°**	Rwy Idg **12000** TDZE **5352** Apt Elev **5434**		ILS or LOC RWY 7 DENVER INTL (DEN)

RNAV-WAAS:

DENVER, COLORADO				16147
WAAS CH **82628** **W16B**	APP CRS **173°**	Rwy Idg **16000** TDZE **5326** Apt Elev **5434**		RNAV (GPS) Y RWY 16R DENVER INTL (DEN)

GBAS:

NEWARK, NEW JERSEY			AL-285 (FAA)	18256
GBAS CH **22727** **G04A**	APP CRS **039°**	Rwy Idg **8460** TDZE **10** Apt Elev **17**		GLS RWY 4L NEWARK LIBERTY INTL (EWR)

FAA Chart Users' Guide - Terminal Procedures Publication (TPP) - Terms

No Primary NAVAID box:

DENVER, COLORADO

APP CRS	Rwy ldg	12000
173°	TDZE	5339
	Apt Elev	5434

16147

RNAV (RNP) Z RWY 17L
DENVER INTL (DEN)

Circling Approach:

ROANOKE, VIRGINIA

VOR ODR	APP CRS	Rwy ldg	N/A
114.9	236°	TDZE	N/A
		Apt Elev	1175

AL-349 (FAA)

16203

VOR/DME-A
ROANOKE-BLACKSBURG RGNL/WOODRUM FLD (ROA)

Sidestep Procedure:

LOS ANGELES, CALIFORNIA

LOC/DME I-OSS	APP CRS		24R	24L
108.5	251°	Rwy ldg	8925	9483
Chan 22		TDZE	120	121
		Apt Elev	126	126

AL-237 (FAA)

16315

ILS or LOC RWY 24R
LOS ANGELES INTL (LAX)

Middle Briefing Strip

The middle briefing strip may contain information in up to three separate boxes, when available, in the following sequence from left to right:

| NOTES BOX | APPROACH LIGHTING SYSTEM | MISSED APPROACH PROCEDURE TEXT BOX |

- **Box 1: Notes Box:** contains procedure notes, Equipment/Requirements Notes box and Takeoff, Alternate, RADAR, WAAS, and/or Cold Weather indicators (details provided below under Notes Box).

- **Box 2: Approach Lighting System Box (when applicable):** shows the approach lighting system name and charting icon. Multiple approach lighting systems may be shown for approaches that have straight-in minimums for parallel runways.

- **Box 3: Missed Approach Procedure Text Box:** The full textual description of the missed approach procedure is provided here.

Notes Box

Procedure Equipment Requirements Notes Box

Performance-Based Navigation (PBN) Requirements and ground-based Equipment Requirements are displayed in separate, standardized notes boxes. For procedures with PBN elements, the PBN box contains the procedure's navigation specification(s). If required, specific sensors or infrastructure needed for the navigation solution, additional or advanced functional requirements, and the minimum Required Navigation Performance (RNP) value and any amplifying remarks will also be included. Items listed in this PBN box are REQUIRED. The separate Equipment Requirements Box will list ground-based equipment requirements.

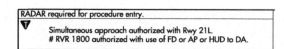

FAA Chart Users' Guide - Terminal Procedures Publication (TPP) - Terms

On procedures with both PBN elements and ground-based equipment requirements, the PBN requirements box is listed first.

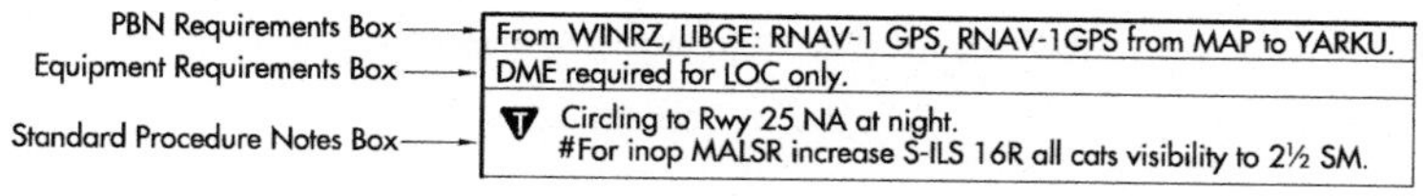
PBN Requirements Box
Equipment Requirements Box
Standard Procedure Notes Box
From WINRZ, LIBGE: RNAV-1 GPS, RNAV-1GPS from MAP to YARKU.
DME required for LOC only.
Circling to Rwy 25 NA at night.
#For inop MALSR increase S-ILS 16R all cats visibility to 2½ SM.

Notes Symbols

Several different symbols may appear within the Notes Box:

T	An entry is published in the Takeoff Minimums, (Obstacle) Departure Procedures, and Diverse Vector Area (Radar Vectors) section of the TPP.
A	Non-standard IFR alternate minimums exist. Refer to IFR Alternate Airport Minimums section of the TPP.
A NA	Alternate minimums are not authorized due to unmonitored facility or absence of weather reporting service.
W	WAAS (Wide Area Augmentation System)
-12°C	Cold Temperature Airport

The negative W within a black square box symbol shown in the Notes section below any "A" or "T" Symbol indicates that outages of the WAAS (Wide Area Augmentation System) vertical guidance may occur daily at this location due to initial system limitations. WAAS NOTAMs for vertical outages are not provided for this approach. Use LNAV minima for flight planning at these locations, whether as a destination or alternate. For flight operations at these locations, when the WAAS avionics indicate that LNAV/VNAV or LPV service is available, then vertical guidance may be used to complete the approach using the displayed level of service. Should an outage occur during the procedure, reversion to LNAV minima may be required.

When -12°C appears in the Notes section below all other symbols it indicates a cold temperature altitude correction is required at that airport when the reported temperature is at or below the published temperature. Advise ATC with altitude correction. Advising ATC with altitude corrections is not required in the final segment. See Aeronautical Information Manual (AIM), Chapter 7, for guidance and additional information. For a complete list of cold temperature airports, see https://aeronav.faa.gov/d-tpp/Cold_Temp_Airports.pdf.

When "ASR", "PAR" or "ASR/PAR" appear in the Note section immediately below the "T" and "A" symbols it indicates there are published Radar Instrument Approach Minimums. Where radar is approved for approach control service, it is used not only for radar approaches (Airport Surveillance Radar [ASR] and Precision Approach Radar [PAR]) but is also used to provide vectors in conjunction with published non-radar approaches based on radio NAVAIDs (ILS, VOR, NDB, TACAN). Radar vectors can provide course guidance and expedite traffic to the final approach course of any established IAP or to the traffic pattern for a visual approach.

Bottom Briefing Strip (Communications Information)

The communications briefing strip contains communication information when available, in separate boxes, listed from left to right in the order that they would be used during arrival with the tower frequency box bolded:

ATIS	APP CON	TOWER	GND CON	CLNC DEL	UNICOM
XXXXX	XXXX XXXX	**XXXX XXXX**	XXXXX	XXXXX	XXXXX

- ATIS, AFIS (AK Only) or ASOS/AWOS frequencies (when available, ATIS or AFIS will be the only weather frequency/s published)
- The primary Approach Control (APP CON) name and frequencies; when the primary approach service is provided by other than Approach Control, e.g. FSS (Radio), Tower, Center, the appropriate air traffic facility call name is provided.
- The Control Tower (TOWER) name and frequencies, to include Precision Radar Monitoring (PRM) and frequency
- Ground Control (GND CON) frequencies
- Clearance Delivery (CLNC DEL) frequencies; where a Control Tower does not exist or is part-time, a remoted CLNC DEL may be listed.
- Ground Communications Outlet (GCO) frequency
- Common Traffic Advisory Frequency (CTAF), shown in parentheses when shares a frequency, e.g. UNICOM 122.8 (CTAF)
- UNICOM or AUNICOM frequency
- Controller Pilot Data Link Communication (CPDLC)

Note: Part-time operations will be annotated with a star. Check Chart Supplement for times of operation.

PLANVIEW

The planview of the IAP charts provides an overhead view of the entire instrument approach procedure.

The data on the planview is shown to scale, unless concentric rings, scale breaks or an inset have been used.

Planview Items

Approach Segments
NAVAIDs
Area Navigation (RNAV) Waypoints
Restrictive Airspeeds
Restrictive Altitudes
Holding Patterns and Procedure Turns
Airports
Relief (Terrain Features)

Hydrography
International Boundary
Obstacles (Man-made, Terrain and Vegetation)
Special Use Airspace
Minimum Safe Altitude
Terminal Arrival Areas
Helicopter (Copter) Procedures

Approach Segments

The planview includes a graphical depiction of procedure entry through missed approach.

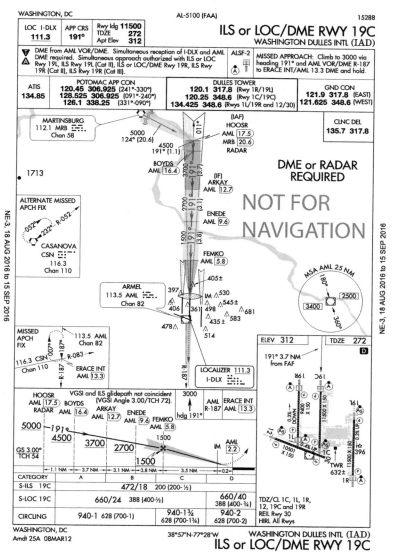

Simple IAP Example

Legend

| Feeder Route | Initial Approach | Intermediate Approach | Final Approach Course | Missed Approach |

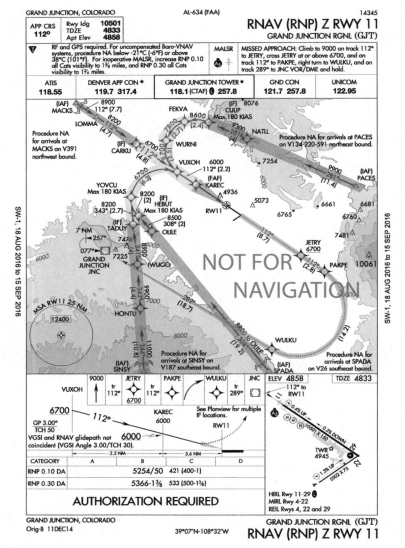

Complex IAP Example with RF Legs

- **Feeder Routes** (highlighted in blue - See Simple IAP Example on previous page) may be used to provide a transition from the enroute structure to the IAF.

- **Initial Approach** (highlighted in purple in examples above) is the segment between the initial approach fix (IAF) and the intermediate fix (IF) or the point where the aircraft is established on the intermediate course or final approach course.

- **Intermediate Approach** (highlighted in yellow in examples above) is the segment between the intermediate fix or point and the final approach fix.

- **Final Approach Course** (highlighted in red in the examples above) is the segment between the final approach fix or point and the runway, airport, or missed approach point.

- **Missed Approach** (highlighted in green in the example above) begins at the MAP and continues until the designated fix or waypoint. Missed Approach Procedure Track is shown as a hash marked line in the planview. If the missed approach fix falls outside of the area of the planview it will be shown in a separate box in the planview.

- **DME arcs or Radius-to-Fix legs (RF)** are shown as smooth arcs from a designated start point to a designated terminus.

FAA Chart Users' Guide - Terminal Procedures Publication (TPP) - Terms

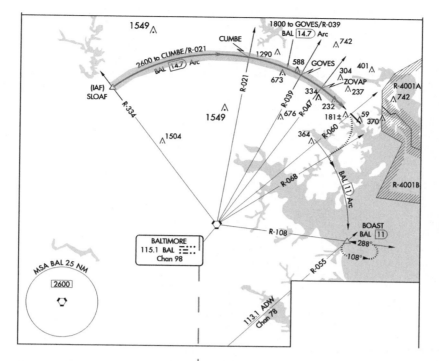

- **Visual segment -** Instrument approach procedures, including Copter approach procedures, that terminate or have missed approaches prior to the airport/heliport, and are authorized to proceed visually, will depict the visual flight path by a dashed line symbol from the missed approach point to the airport.

  On RNAV charts where the visual track may only apply to a specific line of minima, the visual procedure track line will not be shown in the planview. There will be a note directed to that portion of the procedure track.

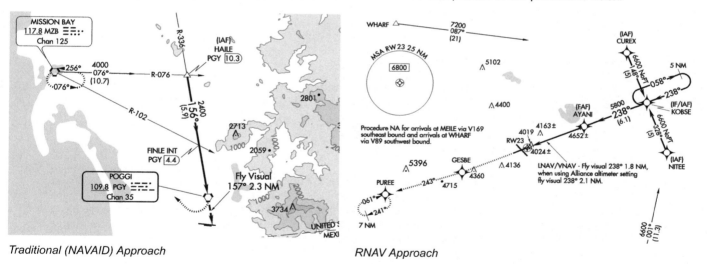

Traditional (NAVAID) Approach   *RNAV Approach*

NAVAIDs

NAVAIDs used on ground based charts will show the appropriate symbol accompanied by a data box that contains the facility name, frequency, identifier and Morse code. A NAVAID box with a heavy line indicates the primary NAVAID used for the approach.

101

NAVAIDs used on GPS based charts show the appropriate symbol identified with the name and identifier.

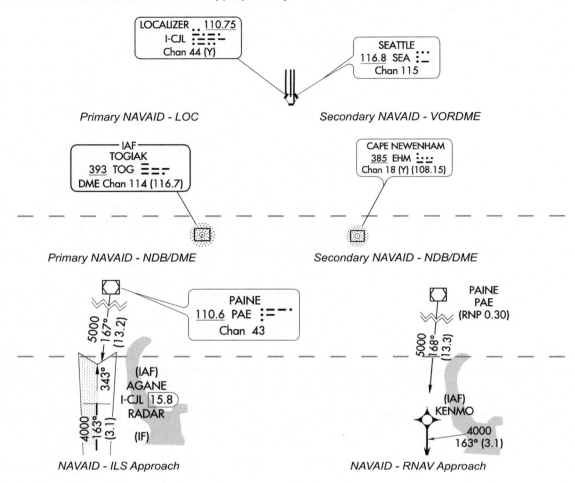

Area Navigation (RNAV) Waypoints

Waypoints are shown with the waypoint symbol accompanied by the five letter identifier. If an RNAV waypoint is collocated with an intersection, DME fix, or NAVAID, the appropriate Intersection, DME fix, or NAVAID symbol will be charted.

ELIZE

On RNAV (RNP) charts, any requirement/capability notes are depicted below the fix/waypoint/NAVAID name. When the required RNP lateral accuracy value for any approach segment other than final approach (e.g. feeder, initial and/or intermediate or missed) are less than standard (RNP 2.00 for feeder, RNP 1.00 for initial and/or intermediate and missed), a note stating the required RNP value may be placed adjacent to the applicable fix at the beginning of the Feeder Route (or annotated in the PBN box). If there is more than one lateral accuracy value within these portions of the procedure, the lowest value is annotated. These notes will take the form "RNP 0.XX, or Min RNP 0.XX" and will be located in close proximity to the relevant fix name (or be identified in the PBN Box).

SHNON
(RNP 0.50)

Localizer Depiction

The localizer is depicted in the Planview using the following symbol. The size of the charted localizer symbol does not serve as an indication of the service volume.

Localizer (LOC/LDA) Course
Right side shading- Front course; Left side shading- Back Course

Restrictive Airspeeds Along the Procedure Track

Restrictive airspeeds along the procedure track are shown paired with their respective fix/facility.

Type	Description	Example
Recommended Speed	Recommended speed is depicted with no lines above or below it	180K
Minimum Speed	Minimum speed is depicted as a number with a line below it	120K
Maximum Speed	Maximum speed is depicted as a number with a line above it	250K
Mandatory Speed	Mandatory speed is depicted as a number with a line above and below it	175K

Altitudes

Restrictive altitudes along the procedure track are shown paired with their respective fix/ facility. Minimum, Maximum, Mandatory and Recommended Altitudes are shown.

Type	Description	Example
Recommended Altitude	Recommended altitude is depicted with no lines above or below it	3000
Minimum Altitude	Minimum altitude is depicted as a number with a line below it	2500
Maximum Altitude	Maximum altitude is depicted as a number with a line above it	4300
Mandatory Altitude	Mandatory altitude is depicted as a number with a line above and below it	5500
Mandatory Block Altitude	Mandatory block altitude is depicted with a minimum and a maximum altitude.	5000 3000

Altitudes that are shown along a route are minimum altitudes.

Minimum Route Altitude → 2000
155°
(15.1)

Holding Patterns and Procedure Turns

Holding Patterns are used for many reasons, including deteriorating weather or high traffic volume. Holding might also be required following a missed approach. Each holding pattern has a fix, a direction to hold from the fix, and an airway, bearing, course, radial, or route on which the aircraft is to hold. These elements, along with the direction of the turns, define the holding pattern. Holding Patterns may not always be depicted to scale.

Missed Approach   Hold In-Lieu of Procedure Turn   Arrival

If a holding pattern has a non-standard speed restriction, it will be depicted by an icon with the limiting air speed shown inside the holding pattern symbol. These elements, along with the direction of the turns, define the holding pattern. If two types of holds are located at the same point, the procedural holding pattern will be shown in-lieu of arrival or missed approach holding patterns. Timing or distance limits for Hold-in-lieu of Procedure Turn Holding Patterns will be shown.

FAA Chart Users' Guide - Terminal Procedures Publication (TPP) - Terms

Waypoints designated as a holding fix are shown as fly-by, without the circle around the symbol. However, in the event the holding fix/waypoint is also designated in some other part of the procedure (i.e., IAF) with a fly-over function, then the holding fix/waypoint will be charted as a fly-over point.

A procedure turn (PT) is the maneuver prescribed to perform a course reversal to establish the aircraft inbound on an intermediate or final approach course. The procedure turn or hold-in-lieu-of procedure turn is a required maneuver when it is depicted on the approach chart. However, the procedure turn or the hold-in-lieu-of PT is not permitted when the symbol "NoPT" is depicted on the initial segment being flown, when a RADAR VECTOR to the final approach course is provided, or when conducting a timed approach from a holding fix. The procedure turn will be shown in the planview and in the profile of the chart. In the planview, the tip of the procedure turn barb is shown at the procedure turn limit, e.g., 10 NM, 15 NM. Users should be aware that it is possible for there to be a terminal/feeder fix along the procedure track that is not associated with the procedure turn. Fixes associated with the procedure turn are depicted in the profile.

Airports

The primary approach airport is shown to scale by a pattern of all the runways. Airports other than the primary approach airport may be shown with an airport pattern and name when in close proximity to the primary airport.

Relief (Terrain Features)

Terrain is depicted in the planview portion of all IAPs at airports that meet the following criteria:

- If the terrain within the planview exceeds 4,000 feet above the airport elevation, or
- If the terrain within a 6.0 nautical mile radius of the Airport Reference Point (ARP) rises to at least 2,000 feet above the airport elevation.

When an airport meets either of the above criteria, terrain will be charted by use of contours, spot elevations, and gradient tints of brown on all IAPs for that airport. Contour layers will be shown in no more than five brown tints, with consecutively darker tints used for consecutively higher elevation contour layers.

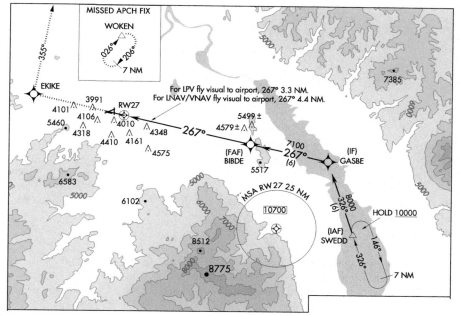

Hydrography (Water)

Water Depiction is depicted in grey, in the planview portion of IAPs. See previous example. The following hydrographic features are shown:

- Oceans
- Significant rivers and streams
- Significant lakes - If only one river or one small lake is involved, not located in the immediate airport vicinity, the hydrographic information requirement may be waived.

International Boundary

When the planview includes a boundary of another country the International boundaries are shown by a dashed line. International boundaries are identified with country name within the country area.

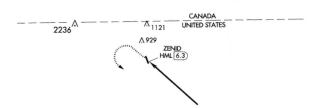

Obstacles (Man-made, Terrain and Vegetation)

Obstacles are shown as △ when they are man-made or vegetation or as a ● when they are terrain. The highest obstacle, whether man-made or terrain is depicted with a bolder and larger symbol along with larger elevation font size. Any obstacle which penetrates a slope of 67:1 emanating from any point along the centerline of any runway shall be considered for charting within the area shown to scale. Obstacles specifically identified by the approving authority for charting shall be charted regardless of the 67:1 requirement.

Unverified obstacles shall be indicated by a doubtful accuracy symbol ± following the elevation value.

On non-precision approaches, obstacles should be considered when determining where to begin descent from the MDA.

FAA Chart Users' Guide - Terminal Procedures Publication (TPP) - Terms

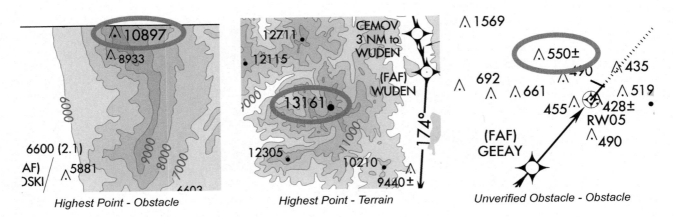

| Highest Point - Obstacle | Highest Point - Terrain | Unverified Obstacle - Obstacle |

Special Use Airspace (SUA)

SUAs consists of that airspace wherein activities must be confined because of their nature, or wherein limitations are imposed upon aircraft operations that are not a part of those activities, or both. These are prohibited areas, restricted areas, warning areas, Military Operations Areas (MOAs), and alert areas. SUA that falls within the area of coverage of the instrument approach procedure chart are shown only when designated by the approving authority.

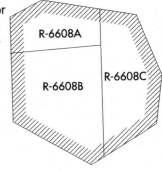

Air Defense Identification Zone (ADIZ)

ADIZ is an area of airspace in which the identification, location, and control of aircraft is required in the interest of national security. When designated by the approving authority, ADIZ boundaries that fall within the area of coverage of the chart are shown. CONTIGUOUS U.S. ADIZ

Minimum Safe Altitude (MSA)

MSAs are published for emergency use on IAP charts. MSAs appear in the planview of all IAPs except on approaches for which a Terminal Arrival Area (TAA) is used. The MSA is based on the primary NAVAID, waypoint, or airport reference point on which the IAP is predicated. The MSA depiction on the approach chart contains the identifier of the NAVAID/waypoint/airport used to determine the MSA altitudes. MSAs are expressed in feet above mean sea level and normally have a 25 NM radius; however, this radius may be expanded to 30 NM if necessary to encompass the airport landing surfaces. Ideally, a single sector altitude is established and depicted on the planview of approach charts; however, when necessary to obtain relief from obstructions, the area may be further sectored and as many as four MSAs established. When established, sectors may be no less than 90° in spread. MSAs provide 1,000 feet clearance over all obstructions but do not necessarily assure acceptable navigation signal coverage.

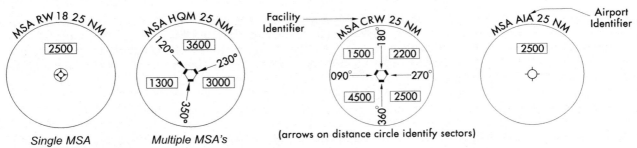

| Single MSA | Multiple MSA's | (arrows on distance circle identify sectors) | |

Terminal Arrival Areas (TAAs)

The TAA icons will be positioned in the planview relative to their relationship to the procedure. The icon will not have feeder routes, airways, or radar vectors depicted. The TAA provides a transition from the enroute structure to the terminal environment with little required pilot/air traffic control interface for aircraft equipped with Area Navigation (RNAV) systems. A standard TAA has three areas: straight-in, left base, and right base. The arc boundaries of the three areas of the TAA are published portions of the approach. A TAA provides minimum altitudes with standard obstacle clearance when operating within the TAA boundaries. TAAs are primarily used on RNAV approaches but may be used on an ILS approach when RNAV is the sole means for navigation to the IF; however, they are not normally used in areas of heavy concentration of air traffic.

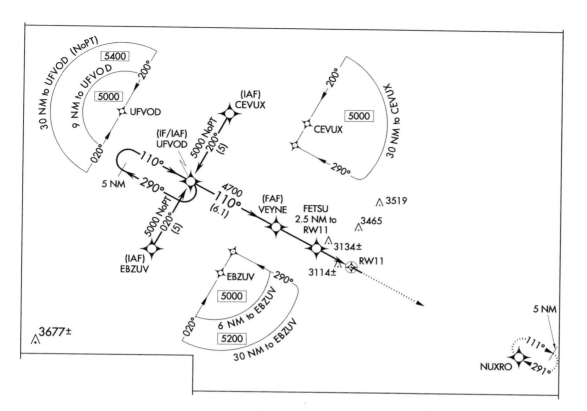

Example of Standard TAA

Non-standard TAAs may also be published; i.e., one base leg, no base legs.

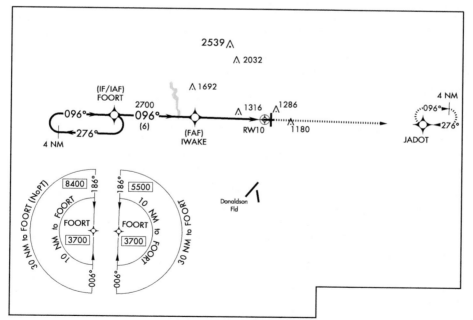

Example of Non-Standard TAA

Helicopter (Copter) Procedures

Copter procedures may contain either a visual or a VFR segment. Visual segments are depicted using the dashed line symbol below.

– – – – ➔

Visual Flight Segment

107

VFR Segments are not depicted with a line, but include the reference bearing and distance information at the endpoint of the VFR Segment, when provided, as shown below.

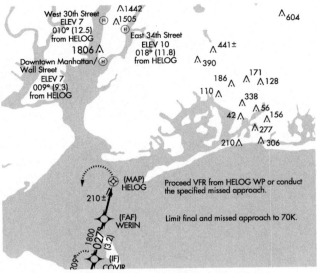

Example of Copter with VFR Segment (JFK)

When a visual flight path or VFR segment is required from the MAP to the heliport or alighting area, and as necessary for an explicit portrayal, an inset of the MAP area may be provided. This MAP area will depict significant landmark visual features. The procedure track, value and distance to the MAP and the visual segment and value to the landing point shall be shown within this inset. If it is a VFR segment, the reference bearing and distance text will be shown at the landing point.

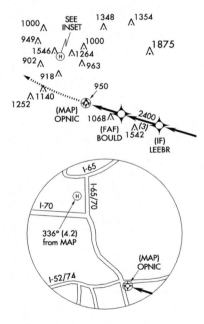

Example of Copter with Inset

MISSED APPROACH INFORMATION

Missed approach information is shown in 3 locations on the chart:

- The Middle Briefing Strip - The complete textual missed approach instructions are provided at the top of the approach chart in the middle pilot briefing strip.

- The Planview - The missed approach track is drawn using a thin, hash marked line with a directional arrow. If the missed approach fix is off the chart, the missed approach track shall extend to the chart border.

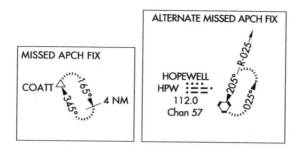

Missed Approach

Missed approach holding patterns that lie outside the geographic parameters of the planview and are unable to be shown with a scale break will be shown as a boxed inset. All alternate missed approach holding patterns will be shown in an inset.

- The Profile Box - Missed Approach Icons will be depicted in the upper left or upper right of the profile box. The Missed Approach Icons are intended to provide quick, at a glance intuitive guidance to the pilot, to supplement the textual missed approach instructions in the briefing strip. Space permitting, all textual missed approach instructions will be graphically depicted in sequence. If space does not permit the depiction of all missed approach icons, only the first four icon boxes will be shown.

Example Missed Approach Icons	Missed Approach Text
13000 ↑ RIL R-250 / TEKGU INT RIL [19] / EKR R-179 / WOKPA EKR [44.2]	MISSED APPROACH: Climb to 13000 on RIL VOR/DME R-250 to TEKGU INT/RIL 19 DME and on EKR VOR/DME R-179 to WOKPA/EKR 44.2 DME and hold, continue climb-in-hold to 13000.
8000 ↘ SVC R-128 / Reverse Course / SVC ⟨⟩	MISSED APPROACH: Climbing left turn to 8000 via SVC R-128, then reverse course to SVC VOR/DME and hold.
9000 ↑ / JETRY tr 112° 6700 / PAKPE tr 112° / ⟶ WULKU / JNC tr 289° ⟨⟩	MISSED APPROACH: Climb to 9000 on track 112° to JETRY, cross JETRY at or above 6700, and on track 112° to PAKPE, right turn to WULKU, and on track 289° to JNC VOR/DME and hold.
14000 ↑ crs 174° / HOMDU ◆ / 160° tr / DEVEC ◆ / 160° tr / FTI ⬡	MISSED APPROACH: Climb to 14000 via 174° course to HOMDU and via 160° track to DEVEC and 160° track to FTI VORTAC and hold.
5800 ↑ / 10000 ↘ hdg 190° / SVC R-193 / KUNRE △	MISSED APPROACH: Climb to 5800, then climbing left turn to 10000 via heading 190° and SVC VOR/DME R-193 to KUNRE INT/SVC VOR/DME 24.1 DME and hold.

PROFILE VIEW

A profile diagram of the instrument approach procedure is shown below the planview. The published descent profile and graphical depiction of the vertical path using those facilities, intersections, fixes, etc. identified in the procedure to the runway are shown. A profile view of the procedure track is shown. The approach track begins toward the top of the primary facility line, unless otherwise dictated by the procedure, and shall descend to where the final approach ends and the missed approach begins.

FAA Chart Users' Guide - Terminal Procedures Publication (TPP) - Terms

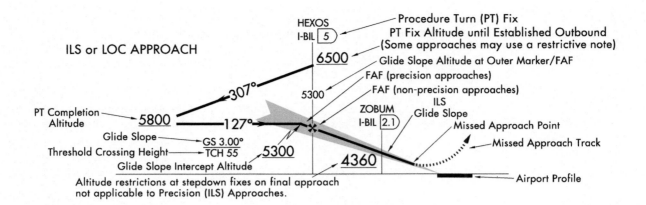

ILS or LOC APPROACH

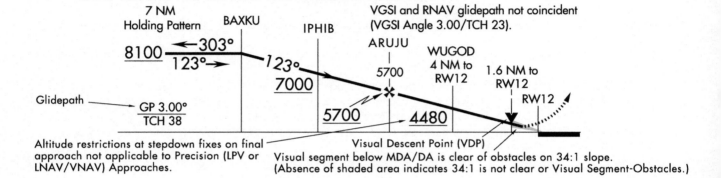

RNAV and GLS PROCEDURES WITH VERTICAL GUIDANCE

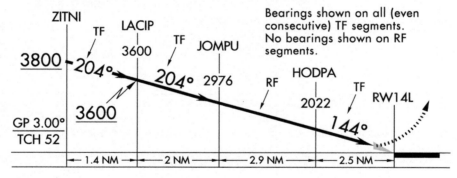

RNP APPROACH WITH TF AND RF SEGMENTS

Precision Approaches

On precision approaches, the glideslope (GS) intercept altitude is illustrated by a zigzag line and an altitude. This is the minimum altitude for GS interception after completion of the procedure turn. Precision approach profiles also depict the GS angle of descent, threshold crossing height (TCH) and GS altitude at the outer marker (OM) or designated fix.

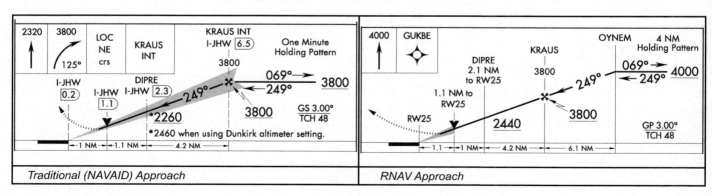

Traditional (NAVAID) Approach | RNAV Approach

Non-Precision Approaches

On non-precision approaches, the final segment begins at the Final Approach Fix (FAF) which is identified with the Maltese cross symbol ✻. When no FAF is depicted, the final approach point is the point at which the aircraft is established inbound on the final approach course. Stepdown fixes may also be provided between the FAF and the airport for authorizing a lower minimum descent angle (MDA) and are depicted with the fix or facility name and a dashed line. Altitude restrictions at stepdown fixes on the final approach on procedures with both precision and non-precision minima are not applicable to precision (ILS, LPV, or LNAV/VNAV) use of the approach. On non-precision only approach procedures, the approach track descends to the MDA or VDP point, thence horizontally to the missed approach point.

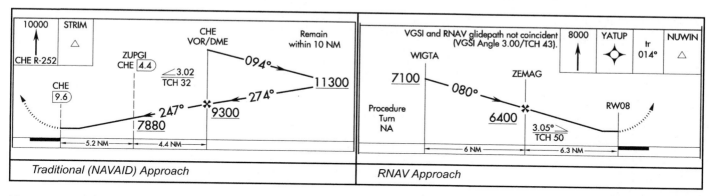

| Traditional (NAVAID) Approach | RNAV Approach |

Visual Decent Point (VDP)

The Visual Descent Point (VDP), is shown by a bold letter "V" positioned above the procedure track and centered on the accompanying dashed line. (See example below.) The VDP is a defined point on the final approach course of a non-precision straight-in approach procedure from which normal descent from the MDA to the runway touchdown point may be commenced.

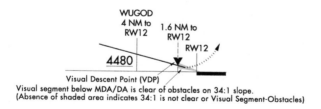

Visual Descent Point (VDP)
Visual segment below MDA/DA is clear of obstacles on 34:1 slope.
(Absence of shaded area indicates 34:1 is not clear or Visual Segment-Obstacles)

Vertical Descent Angle (VDA) and Threshold Crossing Heights (TCH)

A VDA and TCH may be published on non-precision approaches. For Copter approach procedures, a Heliport Crossing Height (HCH) will be depicted in place of the TCH. The VDA is strictly advisory and provides a means to establish a stabilized descent to the MDA. The presence of a VDA does not guarantee obstacle protection in the visual segment. If there are obstacles in the visual segment that could cause an aircraft to destabilize the approach between MDA and touchdown, the profile will not show a VDA and will instead show a note that states "Visual Segment-Obstacles".

FAA Chart Users' Guide - Terminal Procedures Publication (TPP) - Terms

Visual Flight Path

Instrument approach procedures, including Copter approach procedures, that terminate or have missed approaches prior to the airport, and are authorized to proceed visual, shall depict the visual segment by the dashed line symbol from the missed approach point to the airport. The note "Fly visual" ("Proceed visually" on Copter procedures) along with the bearing and distance shall be shown leadered to the visual flight path.

RNAV charts sometimes have visual flight for LNAV/VNAV minima which do not start at the missed approach point. An additional note indicating "LNAV/VNAV" will be placed above the note.

Copter approach procedures with a VFR segment from the missed approach point will not depict the VFR segment with a line in the profile. The note similar to "Proceed VFR from MAP" will be shown.

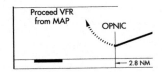

Copter VFR Segment

Chart Examples

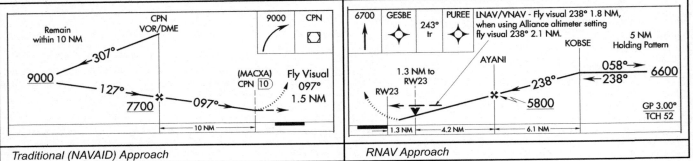

| Traditional (NAVAID) Approach | RNAV Approach |

ILS Glide Slope and RNAV Glidepath

A note providing the glide slope (GS) or glidepath (GP) angle and the threshold crossing height (TCH), are positioned in the lower half of the profile box

- GS will be shown on all ILS procedures.
- GP will be shown GLS procedures and all RNAV procedures with a published decision altitude

Threshold Crossing Height (TCH) has been traditionally used in "precision" approaches as the height of the glide slope above threshold. With publication of LNAV/VNAV minimums and RNAV descent angles, including graphically depicted descent profiles, TCH also applies to the height of the "descent angle," or glidepath, at the threshold.

34:1 Surface Clear Stipple Symbol

On RNAV approach charts, a small shaded arrowhead shaped symbol from the end of the VDA to the runway indicates that the 34:1 Obstacle Clearance Surface (OCS) for the visual segment is clear of obstacles. The absence of the symbol indicates that the 34:1 OCS is not clear or a Visual Segment-Obstacles note is indicated on the chart. (See example in VDP Section.)

LANDING MINIMUMS

The landing minimums section is positioned directly below the profile. This section gives the pilot the lowest altitude and visibility requirements for the approach. There are two types of landing minimums: Straight-in landing or Circling. Straight-in landing minimums are the MDA and visibility, or DA and visibility, required for a straight-in landing on a specified runway. Circling minimums are the MDA and visibility required for the circle-to-land maneuver.

The minimums for straight-in and circling are located under each aircraft category. When there is not a division line between minimums for each category, the minimums apply to two or more categories.

LANDING MINIMA FORMAT

In this example airport elevation is 1179, and runway touchdown zone elevation is 1152.

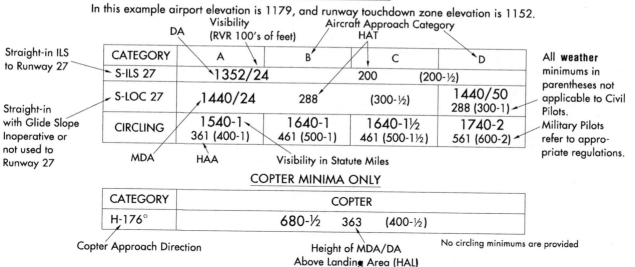

FAA Chart Users' Guide - Terminal Procedures Publication (TPP) - Terms

A second category of straight-in minimums called "sidestep" may be depicted where parallel runways exist.

CATEGORY	A	B	C	D
S-ILS 24R	320/18 200 (200-½)			
S-LOC 24R	460/24 340 (400-½)			460/40 340 (400-¾)
SIDESTEP RWY 24L	580/50 459 (500-1)			580-1½ 459 (500-1½)

The terms used to describe the minimum approach altitudes differ between precision and nonprecision approaches. Precision approaches use DA and nonprecision approaches use MDA, both expressed in feet MSL. The minimum approach altitudes are also referenced to height above touchdown elevation (HAT) for straight-in approaches, or height above airport (HAA) for circling approaches. The figures listed parenthetically are for military operations and are not used in civil aviation.

The visibility values are shown after the DA or MDA. They are provided in statue miles or runway visual range (RVR). RVR is reported in hundreds of feet. If the visibility is in statute miles, there is an altitude number, hyphen, whole or fractional number, e.g. 530-1. This indicates 530 feet MSL and 1 statute mile of visibility. The RVR value is separated from the minimum altitude with a slash, e.g., 1540/24. This indicates 1540 feet MSL and RVR of 2400 feet. When an RVR value is shown, the comparable statute mile equivalent is shown within the military minimums in parentheses as shown in the examples above. This value is determined from the Comparable Values of RVR and Visibility table located in the TPP Legend.

Comparable Values of RVR and Visibility

The following table shall be used for converting RVR to ground or flight visibility. For converting RVR values that fall between listed values, use the next higher RVR value; do not interpolate. For example, when converting 4800 RVR, use 5000 RVR with the resultant visibility of 1 mile.

RVR (feet)	Visibility (SM)	RVR (feet)	Visibility (SM)	RVR (feet)	Visibility (SM)	RVR (feet)	Visibility (SM)
1600	¼	2400	½	3500	⅝	5500	1
1800	½	2600	½	4000	¾	6000	1¼
2000	½	3000	⅝	4500	⅞		
2200	½	3200	⅝	5000	1		

When a reference mark (*, **, #, etc.) is shown on a line of minimums, the qualifying footnote is provided in the notes section.

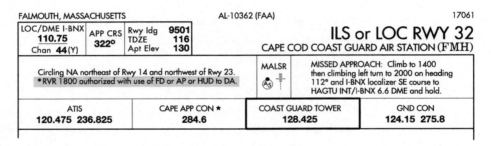

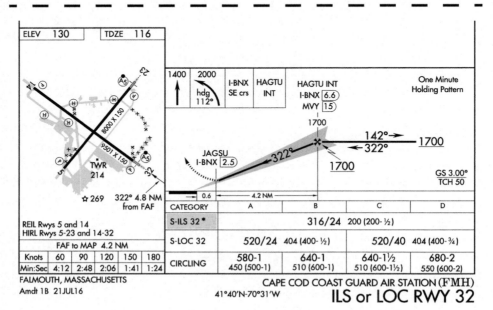

Circling Minimums

There was a change to the TERPS criteria in 2012 that affects circling area dimension by expanding the areas to provide improved obstacle protection. To indicate that the new criteria had been applied to a given procedure, a **C** is placed on the circling line of minimums. The new circling tables and explanatory information is located in the Legend of the TPP.

The approaches using standard circling approach areas can be identified by the absence of the **C** on the circling line of minima.

CATEGORY	A	B	C	D
LPV DA	308/24 200 (200-½)			
LNAV/ VNAV DA	804-2 696 (700-2)			
LNAV MDA	800/24 692 (700-½)		800-1½ 692 (700-1½)	
CIRCLING	800-1 687 (700-1)		800-2 687 (700-2)	860-2½ 747 (800-2½)

Apply Standard Circling Approach Maneuvering Radius Table

CATEGORY	A	B	C	D
C CIRCLING	9120-1¼ 1709 (1800-1¼)	9120-1½ 1709 (1800-1½)	9260-3 1849 (1900-3)	NA

Apply Expanded Circling Approach Maneuvering Airspace Radius Table

FAA Chart Users' Guide - Terminal Procedures Publication (TPP) - Terms

AIRPORT SKETCH

The airport sketch is a depiction of the airport with emphasis on runway pattern and related information, positioned in either the lower left or lower right corner of the chart to aid pilot recognition of the airport from the air and to provide some information to aid on ground navigation of the airport. The runways are drawn to scale and oriented to true north. Runway dimensions (length and width) are shown for all active runways.

Runway(s) are depicted based on what type and construction of the runway.

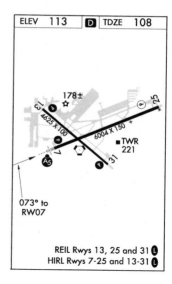

Hard Surface	Other Than Hard Surface	Metal Surface	Closed Runway	Under Construction
■	▦	▨	× ×	⋯⋯
Stopways, Taxiways, Parking Areas	Displaced Threshold	Closed Pavement	Water Runway	
▧	⊕——	x x x	⬚	

Taxiways and aprons are shaded grey. Other runway features that may be shown are runway numbers, runway dimensions, runway slope, arresting gear, and displaced threshold.

Other information concerning lighting, final approach bearings, airport beacon, obstacles, control tower, NAVAIDs, helipads may also be shown.

Airport Elevation and Touchdown Zone Elevation

The airport elevation is shown enclosed within a box in the upper left corner of the sketch box and the touchdown zone elevation (TDZE) is shown in the upper right corner of the sketch box. The airport elevation is the highest point of an airport's usable runways measured in feet from mean sea level. The TDZE is the highest elevation in the first 3,000 feet of the landing surface. Circling only approaches will not show a TDZE.

Runway Declared Distance Information

Runway declared distance information when available will be indicated by **D** and is shown to the right of the airport elevation in the sketch box. Declared distances for a runway represent the maximum distances available and suitable for meeting takeoff and landing distance performance requirements.

Runway Lights

Notes regarding approach lighting systems are shown at the bottom of the sketch box. Runway lights (HIRL) (MIRL) (LIRL) (TDZL)(TDZ/CL) shall be indicated by a note, e.g. HIRL Rwy 9-27.

Other approach lighting is shown on the airport sketch as a symbol on the side of the runway where they are actually located. Symbols that are shown in negative indicate pilot-controlled lighting.

Runway centerline lights (CL) are installed on some precision approach runways to facilitate landing under adverse visibility conditions. They are located along the runway centerline and are spaced at 50 foot intervals. Runways with CL are shown in a negative dot pattern through the middle of the solid runway as illustrated in the airport sketch to right.

Runway centerline lights will be indicated by a note only when paired with TDZL, e.g., TDZ/CL Rwys 6 and 24.

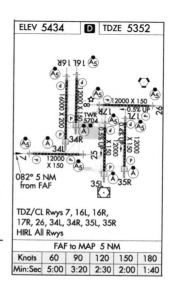

115

FAA Chart Users' Guide - Terminal Procedures Publication (TPP) - Terms

Time/Distance Table

When applicable, a Time/Distance Table is provided below the airport sketch. The table provides the distance and time that is required from the final approach fix to the missed approach point for select groundspeeds.

Base Information (Copter Approaches Only)

Base Information, as required and necessary to identify the MAP area and in the vicinity of the landing area shall be provided. Information shall be limited to and depict significant visual landmark features at and surrounding the MAP area and the heliport/pad of intended landing.

AIRPORT DIAGRAMS

Airport Diagrams are specifically designed to assist in the movement of ground traffic at locations with complex runway/taxiway configurations. Airport Diagrams are not intended for use in approach and landing or departure operations. An airport diagram assists pilots in identifying their location on the airport, thus reducing requests for "progressive taxi instructions" from controllers.

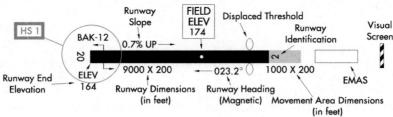

Airport Diagram Features:

1. Runways

   a. Complete with magnetic headings (including magnetic variation and epoch year) and identifiers.
   b. Runways under construction shall also be shown.
   c. Runway dimensions, displaced thresholds, runway end elevations.
   d. Runway surface composition
   e. Weight bearing capacity (landing gear configuration or Pavement Classification Number)
   f. Land and Hold Short (LAHSO) lines, ILS hold lines, Localizer/Glide Slope Critical Areas.
   g. Arresting Gear. To include Engineered Materials Arresting System (EMAS).

2. Taxiways, with identifiers. Taxiways under construction shall also be shown.
3. Hot Spot locations.
4. Parking areas, run-up pads, alert areas, landing pads, "Non-Movement" areas (where pilot is NOT under air traffic control), ramps, aprons and hold pads.
5. Turnarounds, blast pads, stopways, overruns, and clearways (include dimensions when known).
6. Large tanks, including fueling area.
7. Control towers (include tower height).
8. Airport beacon.
9. Helicopter pads.
10. Radar reflectors.
11. Highest obstruction within diagram boundary.
12. Any building that pilot can taxi to. Other buildings to include terminal/administration and Base operations, fire station, NWS, AFSS, FAA, FSDO, ANG, USCG, FBO.
13. Comm Frequencies.

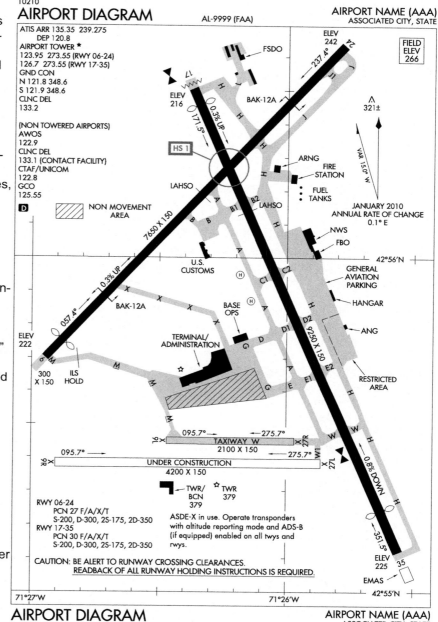

Note: Star when used in the Comm Frequencies indicates part-time status. Check Chart Supplement for times of operation.

Runway Construction

Runway construction is depicted as follows:

Hard Surface	Other Than Hard Surface	Metal Surface	Closed Runway	Under Construction
▮	⬚	▨	⊠ ⊠	⁞⁞⁞
Stopways, Taxiways, Parking Areas	**Displaced Threshold**	**Closed Pavement**	**Water Runway**	
▭	⇳━━	x x x	⌐ ¬	

Hot Spots

Hot Spots (HS) are a runway safety related problem area or intersection on an airport. Typically it is a complex or confusing taxiway/taxiway or taxiway/runway intersection. A confusing condition may be compounded by a miscommunication between a controller and a pilot, and may cause an aircraft separation standard to be compromised. The area may have a history of surface incidents or the potential for surface incidents.

Hot Spots are indicated on the Airport Diagram with a brown open circle or polygon leadered to a Hot Spot number, e.g., HS 1. The number corresponds to a listing and description on the Hot Spot page in the front the TPP. More information and the location of Hot Spots can be found at http://www.faa.gov/airports/runway_safety/hotspots/hotspots_list/.

DEPARTURE PROCEDURES (DPs)

Departure Procedures (DPs) are designed specifically to assist pilots in avoiding obstacles during the climb to the minimum enroute altitude, and/or airports that have civil IFR takeoff minimums other than standard. There are two types of DPs: Obstacle Departure Procedures (ODPs), printed either textually or graphically and Standard Instrument Departures (SIDs), always printed graphically. SIDs are primarily designed for system enhancement and to reduce pilot/controller workload, and require ATC clearance. ODPs provide obstruction clearance via the least onerous route from the terminal area and may be flown without ATC clearance. All DPs provide the pilot with a safe departure from the airport and transition to the enroute structure.

Generally, DP charts are depicted "not to scale" due to the great distances involved on some procedures or route segments. A "to scale" portrayal may be used if readability is assured.

The DP will show the departure routing, including transitions to the appropriate enroute structure. All routes, turns, altitudes, NAVAIDs, facilities forming intersections and fixes, and those facilities terminating the departure route are shown. A textual description of the departure procedure is also provided. For RNAV DPs, the transition text consists of the transition name and associated computer code. On non-RNAV DPs, the transition text will also include the description of all turns, altitudes, radials, bearings and facilities/fixes needed to guide the user from the common departure point to the terminating facility fix.

Copter DPs may also include a visual or VFR segment. Visual segments are depicted using the dashed line symbol below.

— — —➤

Visual Flight Segment

VFR Segments are not depicted with a line, but include the reference bearing and distance information at the endpoint of the VFR Segment, when provided, as shown below.

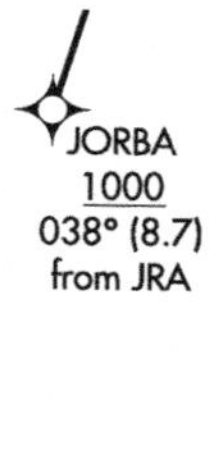

JORBA
1000
038° (8.7)
from JRA

(H)

Example of Copter with VFR Segment

STANDARD TERMINAL ARRIVAL (STARs) CHARTS

STARs are pre-planned Instrument Flight Rule (IFR) air traffic control arrival procedures for pilot use in graphic and/or textual form. STARs depict prescribed routes to transition the aircraft from the enroute structure to a fix in the terminal area from which an instrument approach can be conducted. STARs reduce pilot/controller workload and air-ground communications, minimizing error potential in delivery and receipt of clearances.

STAR charts generally shall be depicted 'not to scale' due to the great distances involved on many procedures and route segments. A 'to scale' depiction may be used only if readability is assured.

The STAR will show the arrival routing, including transitions from the appropriate enroute structure. All routes, turns, altitudes, NAVAIDs, facilities forming intersections and fixes, and those facilities/fixes terminating or beginning the arrival route shall be shown in the graphic depiction. A textual description of the arrival procedure is also provided. For RNAV STARs, transition text will consist of the transition name and associated computer code. For non-RNAV STARs, the transition text will also include a description of all turns, altitudes, radials, bearings and facilities/fixes needed to guide the user from the entry point to the common facility/fix.

CHARTED VISUAL FLIGHT PROCEDURE (CVFP) CHARTS

CVFPs are charted visual approaches established for environmental/noise considerations, and/or when necessary for the safety and efficiency of air traffic operations. The approach charts depict prominent landmarks, courses, and recommended altitudes to specific runways. CVFPs are designed to be used primarily for turbojet aircraft. CVFPs are not instrument approaches and do not have missed approach segments.

CVFPs are named for the primary landmark and the specific runway for which the procedure is developed, such as: RIVER VISUAL RWY 18, STADIUM VISUAL RWY 24. The CVFP charts are divided into planview and notes sections separated by a bar scale in 1 NM increments. The planview of the CVFP includes the portrayal of visual approach procedures information, such as landmarks, NAVAIDs, visual track, hydrography, special use airspace and cultural features, as applicable.

CVFPs originate at or near, and are designed around, prominent visual landmarks and typically do not extend beyond 15 flight path miles from the landing runway. Visual tracks start at a geographical point or landmark where the procedure must be flown visually to the airport. The visual track is indicated by a dashed line. Visual tracks may include the track value, distance and minimum or recommended altitudes.

U.S. TERMINAL PROCEDURES PUBLICATION SYMBOLS

GENERAL INFORMATION

Symbols shown are for the Terminal Procedures Publication (TPP) which includes Standard Terminal Arrival (STARs) Charts, Departure Procedures (DPs), Instrument Approach Procedures (IAP) and Airport Diagrams.

PLANVIEW SYMBOLS

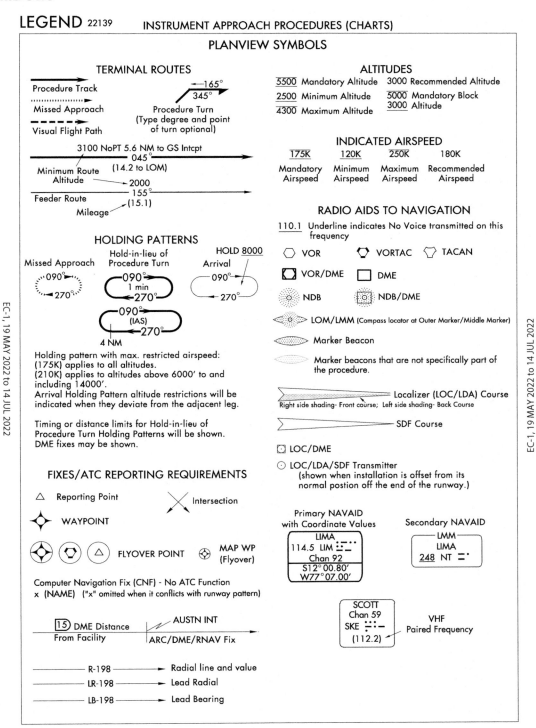

PLANVIEW SYMBOLS (Continued)

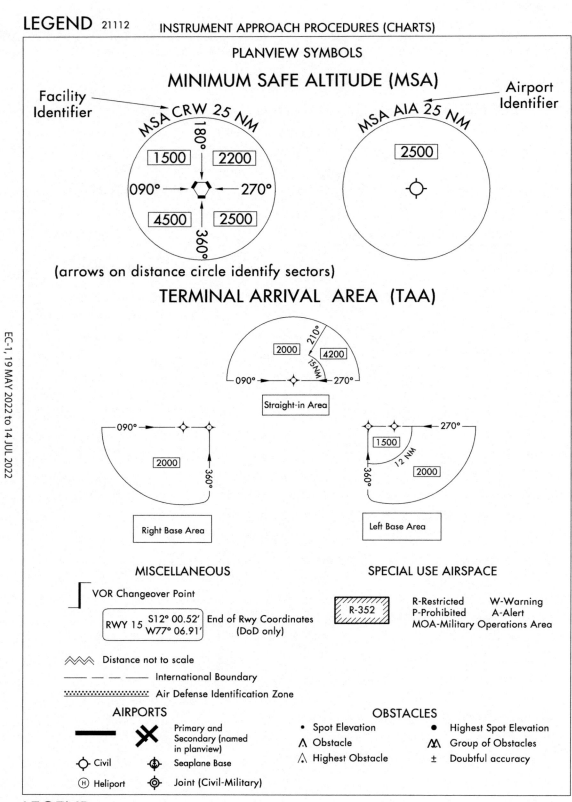

PLANVIEW SYMBOLS

MINIMUM SAFE ALTITUDE (MSA)

Facility Identifier

Airport Identifier

(arrows on distance circle identify sectors)

TERMINAL ARRIVAL AREA (TAA)

Straight-in Area

Right Base Area

Left Base Area

MISCELLANEOUS

VOR Changeover Point

RWY 15 S12° 00.52' End of Rwy Coordinates
        W77° 06.91' (DoD only)

〰〰〰 Distance not to scale

— — — — International Boundary

░░░░░░░░ Air Defense Identification Zone

SPECIAL USE AIRSPACE

R-352

R-Restricted   W-Warning
P-Prohibited   A-Alert
MOA-Military Operations Area

AIRPORTS

✕ Primary and Secondary (named in planview)

◇ Civil

Ⓗ Heliport

⊕ Seaplane Base

◈ Joint (Civil-Military)

OBSTACLES

• Spot Elevation

⋀ Obstacle

⋀ Highest Obstacle

● Highest Spot Elevation

⋀⋀ Group of Obstacles

± Doubtful accuracy

FAA Chart Users' Guide - Terminal Procedures Publication (TPP) - Symbols

EC-1, 19 MAY 2022 to 14 JUL 2022

EC-1, 19 MAY 2022 to 14 JUL 2022

PROFILE VIEW

PROFILE VIEW

Three different methods are used to depict either electronic or vertical guidance: "GS", "GP", or "VDA".

1. "GS" indicates that an Instrument Landing System (ILS) electronic glide slope (a ground antenna) provides vertical guidance. The profile section of ILS procedures depict a GS angle and TCH in the following format: $\frac{GS\ 3.00°}{TCH\ 55}$

2. "GP" on GLS and RNAV procedures indicates that either electronic vertical guidance (via Wide Area Augmentation System - WAAS or Ground Based Augmentation System - GBAS) or barometric vertical guidance is provided. GLS and RNAV procedures with a published decision altitude (DA/H) depict a GP angle and TCH in the following format: $\frac{GP\ 3.00°}{TCH\ 50}$

3. An advisory vertical descent angle (VDA) is provided on non-vertically guided conventional procedures and RNAV procedures with only a minimum descent altitude (MDA) to assist in preventing controlled flight into terrain. On Civil (FAA) procedures, this information is placed above or below the procedure track following the fix it is based on. Absence of a VDA or a note that the VDA is not authorized indicates that the prescribed obstacle clearance surface is not clear and the VDA must not be used below MDA. VDA is depicted in the following format: $\frac{\angle\ 3.00°}{TCH\ 55}$. On Copter procedures this is depicted in the following format: $\frac{\angle\ 7.30°}{HCH\ 20}$

ILS or LOC APPROACH

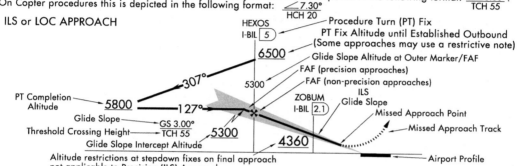

RNAV and GLS PROCEDURES WITH VERTICAL GUIDANCE

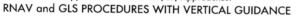

NON-VERTICALLY GUIDED CONVENTIONAL PROCEDURES AND RNAV PROCEDURES WITH MDA ONLY

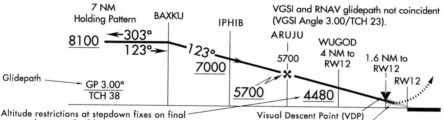

DESCENT FROM HOLDING PATTERN

RNP APPROACH WITH TF AND RF SEGMENTS

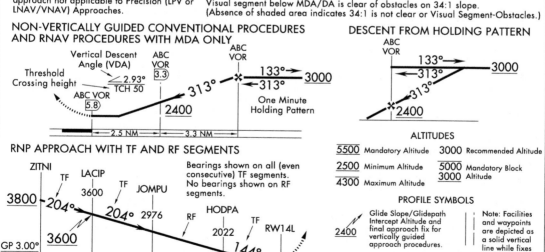

Bearings shown on all (even consecutive) TF segments. No bearings shown on RF segments.

ALTITUDES

<u>5500</u>	Mandatory Altitude	3000	Recommended Altitude
<u>2500</u>	Minimum Altitude	$\overline{5000}$ $\underline{3000}$	Mandatory Block Altitude
$\overline{4300}$	Maximum Altitude		

PROFILE SYMBOLS

24̂00	Glide Slope/Glidepath Intercept Altitude and final approach fix for vertically guided approach procedures.	⋮	Note: Facilities and waypoints are depicted as a solid vertical line while fixes and intersections are depicted as a dashed vertical line.
▼	Visual Descent Point (VDP)		
- - -▶	Visual Flight Path		

EC-1, 19 MAY 2022 to 14 JUL 2022

FAA Chart Users' Guide - Terminal Procedures Publication (TPP) - Symbols

EC-1, 19 MAY 2022 to 14 JUL 2022

STANDARD TERMINAL ARRIVAL (STAR) CHARTS

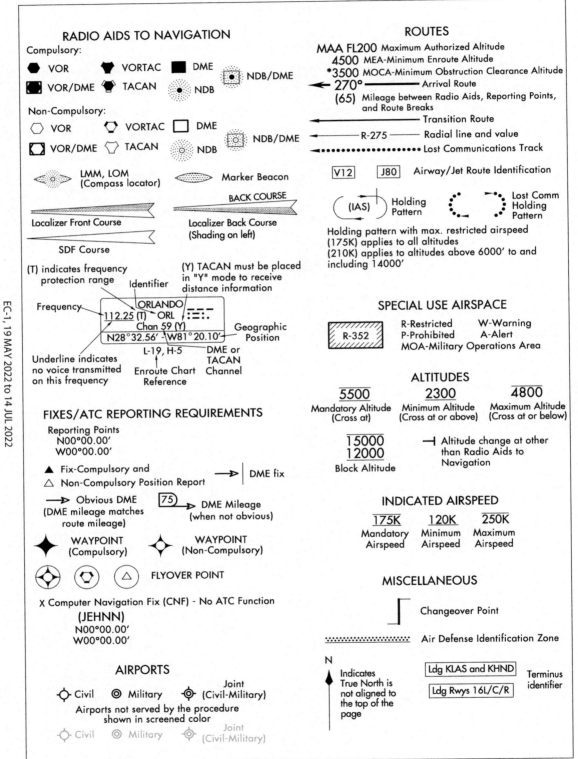

RADIO AIDS TO NAVIGATION

Compulsory:

- ⬢ VOR
- ⬟ VORTAC
- ■ DME
- ⬚ NDB/DME
- ◩ VOR/DME
- ⬠ TACAN
- ● NDB

Non-Compulsory:

- ⬡ VOR
- ⬡ VORTAC
- □ DME
- ▢ NDB/DME
- ◪ VOR/DME
- ⬠ TACAN
- ○ NDB

LMM, LOM (Compass locator)

Marker Beacon

Localizer Front Course

BACK COURSE
Localizer Back Course (Shading on left)

SDF Course

(T) indicates frequency protection range

Identifier

(Y) TACAN must be placed in "Y" mode to receive distance information

Frequency

ORLANDO   ORL ═:═:═
112.25 (T)
Chan 59 (Y)
N28°32.56' W81°20.10'
L-19, H-5

Geographic Position

DME or TACAN Channel

Underline indicates no voice transmitted on this frequency

Enroute Chart Reference

FIXES/ATC REPORTING REQUIREMENTS

Reporting Points
N00°00.00'
W00°00.00'

- ▲ Fix-Compulsory and
- △ Non-Compulsory Position Report
- ⟶ DME fix

- ⟶ Obvious DME (DME mileage matches route mileage)
- 75⟶ DME Mileage (when not obvious)

- ◆ WAYPOINT (Compulsory)
- ◇ WAYPOINT (Non-Compulsory)

- ⊕ ⬡ △ FLYOVER POINT

X Computer Navigation Fix (CNF) - No ATC Function
(JEHNN)
N00°00.00'
W00°00.00'

AIRPORTS

- ◇ Civil
- ◉ Military
- ◈ Joint (Civil-Military)

Airports not served by the procedure shown in screened color

- ◇ Civil
- ◎ Military
- ◈ Joint (Civil-Military)

ROUTES

MAA FL200 Maximum Authorized Altitude
4500 MEA-Minimum Enroute Altitude
*3500 MOCA-Minimum Obstruction Clearance Altitude
⟵ 270° ─── Arrival Route
(65) Mileage between Radio Aids, Reporting Points, and Route Breaks
⟵ ─── Transition Route
⟵ R-275 ─── Radial line and value
•••••••• Lost Communications Track

V12   J80   Airway/Jet Route Identification

(IAS) Holding Pattern

Lost Comm Holding Pattern

Holding pattern with max. restricted airspeed
(175K) applies to all altitudes
(210K) applies to altitudes above 6000' to and including 14000'

SPECIAL USE AIRSPACE

R-352
R-Restricted   W-Warning
P-Prohibited   A-Alert
MOA-Military Operations Area

ALTITUDES

5500 Mandatory Altitude (Cross at)
2300 Minimum Altitude (Cross at or above)
4800 Maximum Altitude (Cross at or below)

15000
12000
Block Altitude

⌐ Altitude change at other than Radio Aids to Navigation

INDICATED AIRSPEED

175K Mandatory Airspeed
120K Minimum Airspeed
250K Maximum Airspeed

MISCELLANEOUS

⌐ Changeover Point

•••••••••••• Air Defense Identification Zone

N ◆ Indicates True North is not aligned to the top of the page

Ldg KLAS and KHND   Terminus identifier
Ldg Rwys 16L/C/R

FAA Chart Users' Guide - Terminal Procedures Publication (TPP) - Symbols
EC-1, 19 MAY 2022 to 14 JUL 2022
EC-1, 19 MAY 2022 to 14 JUL 2022

DEPARTURE PROCEDURE (DP) CHARTS

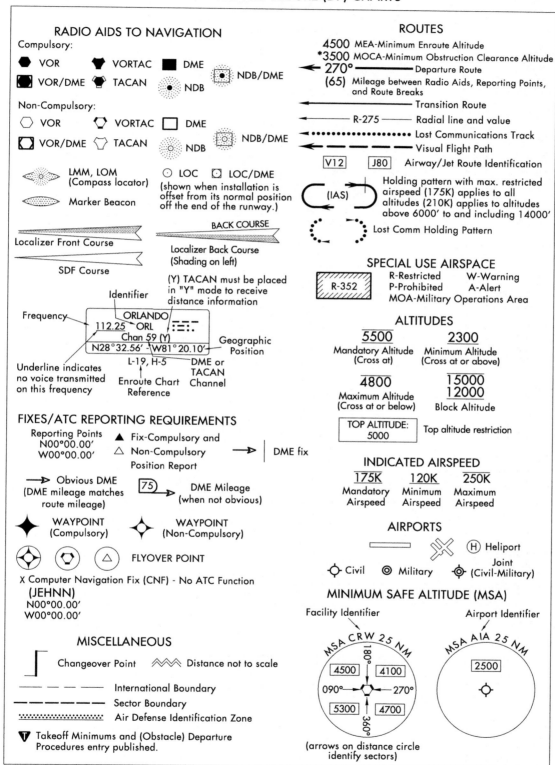

RADIO AIDS TO NAVIGATION

Compulsory:

- ⬢ VOR
- ⬟ VORTAC
- ◼ DME
- ⊡ NDB/DME
- ◨ VOR/DME
- ⬠ TACAN
- ⦿ NDB

Non-Compulsory:

- ⬡ VOR
- ⬠ VORTAC
- ☐ DME
- ⊡ NDB/DME
- ◨ VOR/DME
- ⬠ TACAN
- ◌ NDB

- ◇ LMM, LOM (Compass locator)
- ◉ LOC   ⊡ LOC/DME (shown when installation is offset from its normal position off the end of the runway.)
- ◇ Marker Beacon

Localizer Front Course

BACK COURSE
Localizer Back Course (Shading on left)

SDF Course

(Y) TACAN must be placed in "Y" mode to receive distance information

Frequency — Identifier

| ORLANDO |
| 112.25 ORL ⚏ |
| Chan 59 (Y) |
| N28°32.56' - W81°20.10' |
| L-19, H-5 |

Geographic Position

DME or TACAN Channel

Underline indicates no voice transmitted on this frequency

Enroute Chart Reference

FIXES/ATC REPORTING REQUIREMENTS

Reporting Points
N00°00.00'
W00°00.00'

▲ Fix-Compulsory and
△ Non-Compulsory Position Report

→| DME fix

→ Obvious DME (DME mileage matches route mileage)

[75]→ DME Mileage (when not obvious)

◆ WAYPOINT (Compulsory)

◇ WAYPOINT (Non-Compulsory)

⊕ ⬡ △ FLYOVER POINT

X Computer Navigation Fix (CNF) - No ATC Function

(JEHNN)
N00°00.00'
W00°00.00'

MISCELLANEOUS

⌐ Changeover Point   ⌵⌵⌵ Distance not to scale

— — — International Boundary

— — — — Sector Boundary

⋯⋯⋯⋯ Air Defense Identification Zone

▼ Takeoff Minimums and (Obstacle) Departure Procedures entry published.

ROUTES

- 4500 MEA-Minimum Enroute Altitude
- *3500 MOCA-Minimum Obstruction Clearance Altitude
- ← 270° ——— Departure Route
- (65) Mileage between Radio Aids, Reporting Points, and Route Breaks
- ← ——— Transition Route
- ← R-275 ——— Radial line and value
- •••••••••••••• Lost Communications Track
- ← – – – Visual Flight Path
- [V12] [J80] Airway/Jet Route Identification

(IAS) ⟲ Holding pattern with max. restricted airspeed (175K) applies to all altitudes (210K) applies to altitudes above 6000' to and including 14000'

⋯⋯ Lost Comm Holding Pattern

SPECIAL USE AIRSPACE

[R-352] R-Restricted   W-Warning
P-Prohibited   A-Alert
MOA-Military Operations Area

ALTITUDES

5500	2300
Mandatory Altitude (Cross at)	Minimum Altitude (Cross at or above)
4800	15000 12000
Maximum Altitude (Cross at or below)	Block Altitude

TOP ALTITUDE: 5000   Top altitude restriction

INDICATED AIRSPEED

| 175K | 120K | 250K |
| Mandatory Airspeed | Minimum Airspeed | Maximum Airspeed |

AIRPORTS

▭   ✕   Ⓗ Heliport

✛ Civil   ◎ Military   ⬙ Joint (Civil-Military)

MINIMUM SAFE ALTITUDE (MSA)

Facility Identifier

MSA CRW 25 NM
180°
4500 | 4100
090° — — 270°
5300 | 4700
360°

Airport Identifier

MSA A1A 25 NM
2500

(arrows on distance circle identify sectors)

EC-1, 19 MAY 2022 to 14 JUL 2022

FAA Chart Users' Guide - Terminal Procedures Publication (TPP) - Symbols

EC-1, 19 MAY 2022 to 14 JUL 2022

FAA Chart Users' Guide - Terminal Procedures Publication (TPP) - Symbols

EC-1, 19 MAY 2022 to 14 JUL 2022

EC-1, 19 MAY 2022 to 14 JUL 2022

22139
LEGEND

INSTRUMENT APPROACH PROCEDURES (CHARTS)

AIRPORT DIAGRAM/AIRPORT SKETCH

Runways

Hard Surface	Other Than Hard Surface	Stopways,Taxiways, Parking Areas	Metal Surface

Closed Runway	Closed Surface	Under Construction	Water Runway

ARRESTING GEAR: Specific arresting gear systems; e.g., BAK12, MA-1A etc., shown on airport diagrams, not applicable to Civil Pilots. Military Pilots refer to appropriate DOD publications.

⌐ uni-directional   ⌐ bi-directional   ≷ Jet Barrier

ARRESTING SYSTEM [   ]   (EMAS)

REFERENCE FEATURES

Displaced Threshold...............................
Hot Spot ....
Runway Holding Position Markings......................
Buildings...
24-Hour Self-Serve Fuel ##...............................
Tanks..
Obstructions.......................................
Airport Beacon #...............................☆ ✪
Runway Radar Reflectors.............................
Bridges..
Control Tower #..............................TWR

When Control Tower and Rotating Beacon are co-located, Beacon symbol will be used and further identified as TWR.

A fuel symbol is shown to indicate 24-hour self-serve fuel available, see appropriate Chart Supplement for information.

NOTE:
All new and revised airport diagrams are shown referenced to the World Geodetic System (WGS) (noted on appropriate diagram), and may not be compatible with local coordinates published in FLIP. (Foreign Only)

Runway Weight Bearing Capacity or Pavement Classification Number (PCN)/Pavement Classification Rating (PCR) is shown as a codified expression. Refer to the appropriate Supplement/Directory for applicable codes e.g., RWY 14-32 PCR 560 R/B/W/T; S-75, D-185, 2S-175, 2D-325

Helicopter Alighting Areas   Ⓗ ⊞ H ⚠ ⊞

Negative Symbols used to identify Copter Procedures landing point....................●Ⓗ ⊞ H ▲ ✚

NOTE:
Landmark features depicted on Copter Approach insets and sketches are provided for visual reference only.

Runway TDZ elevation....................TDZE 123

←0.3% DOWN

Runway Slope..............................0.8% UP→
(shown when rounded runway slope is greater than or equal to 0.3%)

NOTE:
Runway Slope measured to midpoint on runways 8000 feet or longer.

⌧ U.S. Navy Optical Landing System (OLS) "OLS" location is shown because of its height of approximately 7 feet and proximity to edge of runway may create an obstruction for some types of aircraft.

Approach light symbols are shown in the Flight Information Handbook.

Airport diagram scales are variable.

True/magnetic North orientation may vary from diagram to diagram

Coordinate values are shown in 1 or ½ minute increments. They are further broken down into 6 second ticks, within each 1 minute increments.

Positional accuracy within ±600 feet unless otherwise noted on the chart.

Runway length depicted is the physical length of the runway (end-to-end, including displaced thresholds if any) but excluding areas designated as stopways.

A 🄳 symbol is shown to indicate runway declared distance information available, see appropriate Chart Supplement for distance information.

HS 1

Runway Slope   FIELD ELEV 174   Displaced Threshold   Runway Identification   Visual Screen

20   0.7% UP→   •   2

ELEV 164   9000 X 200   ←023.2°   1000 X 200   EMAS

Runway End Elevation   Runway Dimensions (in feet)   Runway Heading (Magnetic)   Movement Area Dimensions (in feet)

SCOPE

Airport diagrams are specifically designed to assist in the movement of ground traffic at locations with complex runway/taxiway configurations. Airport diagrams are not intended to be used for approach and landing or departure operations. For revisions to Airport Diagrams: Consult FAA Order 7910.4.

LEGEND

APPROACH LIGHTING SYSTEM

INSTRUMENT APPROACH PROCEDURES (CHARTS)
APPROACH LIGHTING SYSTEM - UNITED STATES

Approach lighting and visual glide slope systems are indicated on the airport sketch by an identifier, e.g., Ⓐ2, Ⓥ, etc.

A dot "•" portrayed with approach lighting letter identifier indicates sequenced flashing lights (F) installed with the approach lighting system e.g., Ⓐ1. Negative symbology, e.g., Ⓐ1, Ⓥ indicates Pilot Controlled Lighting (PCL).

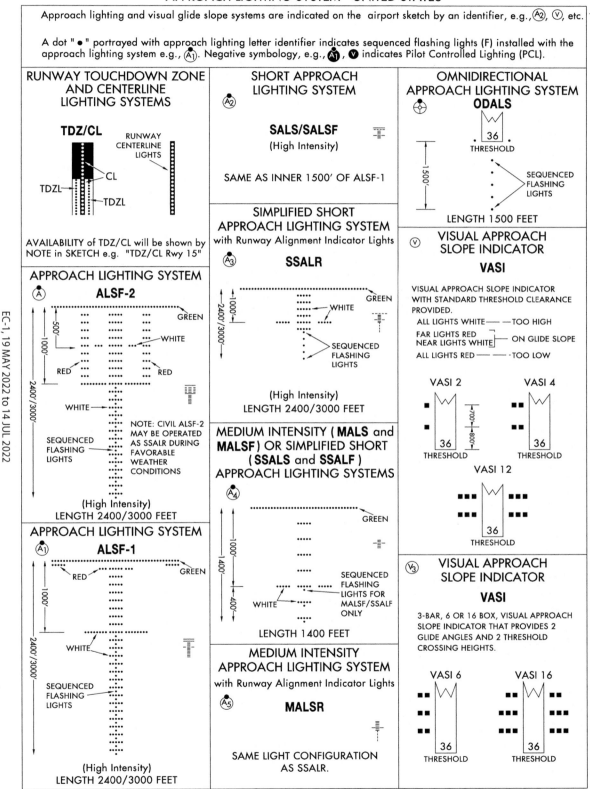

EC-1, 19 MAY 2022 to 14 JUL 2022

EC-1, 19 MAY 2022 to 14 JUL 2022

FAA Chart Users' Guide - Terminal Procedures Publication (TPP) - Symbols

APPROACH LIGHTING SYSTEM (Continued)

FAA Chart Users' Guide - Terminal Procedures Publication (TPP) - Symbols

EC-1, 19 MAY 2022 to 14 JUL 2022

EC-1, 19 MAY 2022 to 14 JUL 2022

LEGEND 22027

INSTRUMENT APPROACH PROCEDURES (CHARTS)
APPROACH LIGHTING SYSTEM - UNITED STATES

Approach lighting and visual glide slope systems are indicated on the airport sketch by an identifier, (A2) , (V) etc.

A dot " ● " portrayed with approach lighting letter identifier indicates sequenced flashing lights (F) installed with the approach lighting system e.g., (A1). Negative symbology, e.g., (A1) , (V) indicates Pilot Controlled Lighting (PCL).

(P) ### PRECISION APPROACH PATH INDICATOR
PAPI

Too low   Slightly low

On correct approach path

Slightly high   Too high

Legend: □ White   ■ Red

(V2) ### PULSATING VISUAL APPROACH SLOPE INDICATOR
PVASI

Pulsating White

Steady White or Alternating Red/White

Above Glide Path
On Glide Path
Slightly Below Glide Path — Steady Red
Below Glide Path — Pulsating Red

Threshold

CAUTION: When viewing the pulsating visual approach slope indicators in the pulsating white or pulsating red sectors, it is possible to mistake this lighting aid for another aircraft or a ground vehicle. Pilots should exercise caution when using this type of system.

(V4) ### TRI-COLOR VISUAL APPROACH SLOPE INDICATOR
TRCV

Above Glide Path — Amber
On Glide Path — Green ← Amber
Below Glide Path — Red

CAUTION: When the aircraft descends from green to red, the pilot may see a dark amber color during the transition from green to red.

(V5)

ALIGNMENT OF ELEMENTS SYSTEMS
APAP

Above glide path   On Glide Path   Below Glide Path

Painted panels which may be lighted at night. To use the system the pilot positions the aircraft so the elements are in alignment.

LEGEND 22027

REFERENCES

There are several references available from the FAA to aid pilots and other interest parties to learn more about FAA Charts and other aspects of aviation.

Publication		FAA Publication ID
	Aeronautical Information Manual (AIM) URL: http://www.faa.gov/air_traffic/publications/	
	Airplane Flying Handbook URL: https://www.faa.gov/regulations_policies/handbooks_manuals/aviation/airplane_handbook/	FAA-H-8083-3A
	Helicopter Flying Handbook URL: http://www.faa.gov/regulations_policies/handbooks_manuals/aviation/helicopter_flying_handbook/	FAA-H-8083-21A
	Instrument Procedures Handbook URL: http://www.faa.gov/regulations_policies/handbooks_manuals/aviation/instrument_procedures_handbook/	FAA-H-8083-16B
	Instrument Flying Handbook URL: http://www.faa.gov/regulations_policies/handbooks_manuals/aviation/media/FAA-H-8083-15B.pdf	FAA-H-8083-15B
	Pilot's Handbook of Aeronautical Knowledge URL: https://www.faa.gov/regulations_policies/handbooks_manuals/aviation/phak/	FAA-H-8083-25B
	Remote Pilot - Small Unmanned Aircraft Systems Study Guide URL: http://www.faa.gov/regulations_policies/handbooks_manuals/aviation/media/remote_pilot_study_guide.pdf	FAA-G-8082-22

ABBREVIATIONS

A

AAF - Army Air Field
AAS - Airport Advisory Service
AAUP - Attention All Users Page
AC - Advisory Circular
ADF - Automatic Direction Finder
ADIZ - Air Defense Identification Zone
ADS - Automatic Dependent Surveillance
ADS-B - Automatic Dependent Surveillance-Broadcast
Advsry - Advisory
AFB - Air Force Base
AFIS - Automatic Flight Information Service
AFS - Air Force Station
AFSS - Automated Flight Service Station
AGL - Above Ground Level
AIM - Aeronautical Information Manual
AIRAC - Aeronautical Information Regulation And Control
AK - Alaska
AL - Approach and Landing
ANG - Air National Guard
APP - Approach
APP CON - Approach Control
APP CRS - Approach Course
Apt - Airport
APV - Approaches with Vertical Guidance
ARP - Airport Reference Point
ARTCC - Air Route Traffic Control Center
ASDA - Accelerate-Stop Distance Available
ASDE-X - Airport Surface Detection Equipment-Model X
ASOS - Automated Surface Observing Station
ASR - Airport Surveillance Radar
ATC - Air Traffic Control
ATIS - Automatic Terminal Information Service
ATS - Air Traffic Service
AUNICOM - Automated Aeronautical Advisory Station
AWOS - Automated Weather Observing Station

B

Baro-VNAV - Barometric Vertical Navigation
BS - Broadcast Station

C

CAC - Caribbean Aeronautical Chart
CAT - Category
CFA - Controlled Firing Areas
CFR - Code of Federal Regulations
CH - Channel
CL - Runway Centerline Lights
CLNC DEL - Clearance Delivery
CNF - Computer Navigation Fix
COP - Changeover Point
CPDLC - Controller Pilot Data Link Communication
CRS - Course
CT - Control Tower

CTAF - Common Traffic Advisory Frequency
CVFP - Charted Visual Flight Procedure
CZ - Control Zone (Canada)

D

DA - Decision Altitude
DA - Density Altitude
D-ATIS - Digital Automatic Terminal Information Service
DH - Decision Height
DME - Distance Measuring Equipment
DND - Department of National Defense (Canada)
DoD - Department of Defense
DOF - Digital Obstacle File
DP - Departure Procedure
DT - Daylight Savings Time
DVA - Diverse Vector Area

E

E - East
EFAS - Enroute Flight Advisory Service
EFB - Electronic Flight Bag
Elev - Elevation
EMAS - Engineered Materials Arresting System

F

FAA - Federal Aviation Administration
FAF - Final Approach Fix
FAP - Final Approach Point
FAR - Federal Aviation Regulation
FBO - Fixed-Based Operator
FIR - Flight Information Region
FL - Flight Level
FLIP - Flight Information Publication
FMS - Flight Management System
FREQ - Frequency
FRZ - Flight Restricted Zone
FSDO - Flight Standards District Office
FSS - Flight Service Station

G

GBAS - Ground-Based Augmentation System
GCO - Ground Communications Outlet
GLS - GBAS Landing System
GND - Ground
GND CON - Ground Control
GNSS - Global Navigation Satellite System
GP - Glide Path
GPS - Global Positioning System
GS - Glide Slope
GS - Ground Speed

H

HAA - Height Above Airport
HAR - High Altitude Redesign
HAT - Height Above Touchdown
HCH - Heliport Crossing Height
HF - High Frequency
HIRL - High Intensity Runway Lights
HS - Hot Spot

I

IAC - Interagency Air Committee
IACC - Interagency Air Cartographic Committee
IAF - Initial Approach Fix
IAP - Instrument Approach Procedure
ICAO - International Civil Aviation Authority
IDT - Identifier
IF - Intermediate Fix
IFR - Instrument Flight Rules
ILS - Instrument Landing System
IMC - Instrument Meteorological Conditions
INS - Inertial Navigation System
IR - Instrument Route (Military)
IRU - Inertial Reference Unit

J

JO - Joint Order

K

KIAS - Knots

L

LAA - Local Airport Advisory
LAAS - Local Area Augmentation System
LAHSO - Land and Hold Short
LDA - Landing Distance Available
LDA - Localizer-type Directional Aid
Ldg - Landing
LF - Low Frequency
LIRL - Low Intensity Runway Lights
LNAV - Lateral Navigation
LOC - Localizer
LOM - Locator Outer Marker
LPV - Localizer Performance with Vertical Guidance
LRRS - Long Range Radar Station
LTP - Landing Threshold Point

M

MAA - Maximum Authorized Altitude
MAP - Missed Approach Point
MCA - Minimum Crossing Altitude
MCAS - Marine Corps Air Station
MDA - Minimum Descent Altitude
MDH - Minimum Descent Height

MEA - Minimum Enroute Altitude
MEF - Maximum Elevation Figure
MF - Medium Frequency
MIA - Minimum IFR Altitude
MIRL - Medium Intensity Runway Lights
MOA - Military Operations Areas
MOCA - Minimum Obstruction Clearance Altitude
MON - Minimum Operational Network
MORA - Minimum Off-Route Altitude
MRA - Minimum Reception Altitude
MSA - Minimum Safe Altitude
MSL - Mean Sea Level
MTA - Minimum Turning Altitude
MTR - Military Training Route
MVA - Minimum Vector Altitude

N

N - North
N/A - Not Applicable
NA - Not Authorized
NAAS - Naval Auxiliary Air Station
NAS - Naval Air Station
NAS - National Airspace System
NAV - Naval Air Facility
NAVAID - Navigational Aid (Ground based)
NDB - Non-Directional Radiobeacon
NextGen - Next Generation Air Transportation System
NFDC - National Flight Data Center
NFPO - National Flight Procedures Office
NM - Nautical Mile
NOAA - National Oceanic and Atmospheric Administration
NO A/G - No Air-to-Ground Communication
NOTAM - Notice to Air Missions, formerly known as Notice to Airmen
NoPT - No Procedure Turn
NPA - Non-Precision Approach
NTAP - Notices to Air Missions Publication
NWS - National Weather Service

O

OAT - Outside Air Temperature
OBS - Omni Bearing Selector
OCA - Ocean Control Area
OCS - Obstacle Clearance Surface
ODP - Obstacle Departure Procedure
OM - Outer Marker
OROCA - Off Route Obstruction Clearance Altitude

P

PA - Precision Approach
PAR - Precision Approach Radar
PBN - Performance-Based Navigation
PRM - Precision Runway Monitor
PT - Procedure Turn
PTP - Point-to-Point
Pvt - Private

R

R - Radial
R - Receive
R - Restricted Area (Special Use Airspace)
RCO - Remote Communications Outlet
RF - Radius-to-Fix
RNAV - Area Navigation
RNP - Required Navigation Performance
RNP AR - Required Navigation Performance Authorization
      Required
ROC - Required Obstacle Clearance
RP - Right Pattern
RVR - Runway Visual Range
RVSM - Reduced Vertical Separation Minimum
Rwy - Runway

S

S - South
SAAAR - Special Aircraft and Aircrew Authorization
      Required
SAAR - Special Aircraft and Aircrew Requirements
SATNAV - Satellite Navigation
SDF - Simplified Directional Facility
SER - Start End of Runway
SFAR - Special Flight Rules Area
SFC - Surface
SFRA - Special Flight Rules Area
SIAPs - Standard Instrument Approach Procedures
SID - Standard Instrument Departure
SM - Statute Mile
SMAR - Special Military Activity Routes
SMGCS - Surface Movement Guidance and Control
      System
SOIA - Simultaneous Offset Instrument Approaches
SSV - Standard Service Volume
STAR - Standard Terminal Arrival Procedure
SUA - Special Use Airspace
SVFR - Special Visual Flight Rules

T

T - Transmit
TA - Travel Advisory
TAA - Terminal Arrival Area
TAC - Terminal Area Chart
TACAN - Tactical Air Navigation
TAS - True Air Speed
TCA - Terminal Control Areas (Canada)
TCH - Threshold Crossing Height
TDZ - Touchdown Zone
TDZE - Touchdown Zone Elevation
TDZL - Touchdown Zone Lights
TDZ/CL - Touchdown Zone/Centerline Lights
TERPS - U.S. Standard for Terminal Instrument Procedures
TFR - Temporary Flight Restriction
TIBS - Telephone Information Briefing Service
TIS-B - Traffic Information Service - Broadcast

TOC - Top of Climb
TOD - Top of Descent
TODA - Takeoff Distance Available
TOGA - Takeoff/Go Around
TORA - Takeoff Runway Available
TPP - Terminal Procedures Publication
TRSA - Terminal Radar Service Area
TWR - Tower

U

UC - Under Construction
UHF - Ultra High Frequency
UIR - Upper Information Region
UNICOM - Universal Communications
U.S. - United States
USA - United States Army
USAF - United States Air Force
USCG - United State Coast Guard
UTA - Upper Control Area

V

VCOA - Visual Climb Over Airport / Airfield
VDA - Vertical Descent Angle
VDP - Visual Decent Point
VFR - Visual Flight Rules
VGSI - Visual Glide Slope Indicator
VHF - Very High Frequency
VMC - Visual Meteorological Conditions
VNAV - Vertical Navigation
VOR - VHF Omnidirectional Radio Range
VORTAC - VHF Omnidirectional Radio Range/Tactical Air
      Navigation
VPA - Vertical Path Angle
VR - Visual Route (Military)

W

W - Warning Area (Special Use Airspace)
W - West
WAAS - Wide-Area Augmentation System
WAC - World Aeronautical Chart
WP - Waypoint
WX CAM - Weather Camera (Alaska)

Printed in Great Britain
by Amazon

80978129R00079